Ethereal Encounter

Amidst an alien expanse, where the very fabric of
reality wavers,
A lone figure stands—a wanderer lost in cosmic
reverie.
The twin suns, their hues divergent, cast their final
embrace,
Painting the horizon in a symphony of cerulean and
crimson.

The air hums with anticipation as if the veil between
worlds thins.
From the shimmering distance, they emerge—the
Others—
Translucent forms, humanoid yet otherworldly,
Their existence is a dance of light and shadow.

Their eyes, like fractured prisms, hold secrets untold,
And their touch, a whisper of forgotten memories.
Do they come as emissaries or harbingers?
Their purpose veiled; their intentions inscrutable.

The lone figure hesitates, heart, echoing in the void.
Is this communion or confrontation?
In the twilight of dual sunsets, destiny unfolds—
A cosmic rendezvous, a collision of realms.

And so they draw near, these spectral wanderers,
Their forms merge with the alien plain.
Will they share wisdom or unravel sanity?
The lone figure stands, poised between worlds.

Praise For . . .

When Spirits Speak: A Cosmic Connection - Discovering Friendships with Star Beings

Arcturian Star Seed, author of spiritual communion and clairvoyant Medium Jeri K. Tory, has again taken us behind the veil. From a detailed explanation of the primary Star Seed races and what planetary systems they are from to an in-depth examination of cross-dimensional communication, alien life on other planets, and what other planets experience in terms of wars, weapons, financial systems, and other daily aspects of alien existence.

This book is riveting as it answers many questions I had myself through an entity known as Zara, with whom Jeri communicates to obtain complex answers to our own spiritual existence and life elsewhere. With so many signs occurring that our present life on planet Earth is in a dire state, the author guides the reader to "peace," knowing there is life elsewhere in our vast multi-dimensional universe. I highly recommend this book to anyone seeking a purpose of existentialism on planet Earth and beyond.

Matthew Douglas Pinard, Author, Angelic Healing Connection and Catholic Mystic

Few people have the privilege of conversing with "Star People," alien beings who are far more advanced than us humans. Jeri K. Tory is one of the few. And fortunately for us, she documents her intimate conversations and thoughtful questions, and their uncensored responses.

This book will give you insights about life, pivotal issues on our planet, and our place in the universe as understood from higher and wiser perspectives. This book is a thesis, a treatise, and a fun read.

Gayla Gordon, Visionary Artist & Author

When Spirits Speak:

A Cosmic Connection - Discovering Friendships with Star Beings

ALSO BY THE AUTHOR

(Formerly – Jeri K. Tory Conklin)

When Spirits Speak: Stiltbird's Last
Supper - A Frequency Interrupted - A
New Beginning (2022)
When Spirits Speak: Messages from
Spirit Children –
2nd Edition (2022)
When Spirits Speak: Stories are Born
(2022)
When Spirits Speak: A Gathering of
Heroes – Cost of Freedom – 2nd Edition
(2023)

Cover Photo:

A lone figure (the author) stands on a vast alien plain bathed in the light of a double sunset (two suns in different colors on the horizon). Strange humanoid figures approach, their forms shimmering and translucent. Dwarfed by the vast alien landscape, their posture conveys a mix of wonder and trepidation. I have been waiting. What about you?

When Spirits Speak:

A Cosmic Connection - Discovering Friendships with Star Beings

Jeri K. Tory, PhD

7th Wave Publishing Prescott Valley, AZ

Paperback ISBN: 979-8-9870717-0-0

Hardcover ISBN: 979-8-9870717-1-7

eBook ISBN: 979-8-9870717-2-4

Printed in the United States of America

Published by: Writer's Publishing House
Prescott, AZ 86301

Cover photo provided by Gayla Gordon

Project Management and Book Launch by Creative Artistic Excellence Marketing
https://creativeartisticexcellence.com

DEDICATION

The Stars
The stars are like jewels in the sky.
They sparkle and shine with their own light.
They are so far away, yet so close to our hearts.
They guide us through the night and fill us with delight.

The stars are like stories in the sky.
They tell us of the past and hint at the future.
They are so ancient, yet so timeless.
They witness our joys and share our sorrows.

The stars are like dreams in the sky.
They challenge us to explore and inspire us to create.
They are so vast, yet so intimate.
They reflect our hopes and reveal our fears.

The stars are like friends in the sky.
They comfort us with their presence and surprise us with their diversity.
They are so different, yet so similar.
They connect us with each other and remind us of ourselves.

This book is dedicated with gratitude and admiration to all the seekers and dreamers who dare to explore the mysteries of the cosmos and the depths of their souls and to the pioneers and visionaries of the cosmic connection who have opened the doors to new realms of possibility and understanding. And to my starborn family and friends, who have shown me the wonders of

the universe and the power of love – Om Namaste –
Kodish, Kodish, Kodoish, Adonai, Tsebayoth[1]

To my beloved friend Gorto, who has been my constant companion and support on this incredible journey—you are my shining star, my soul, my everything.

To my friend Nebula, for igniting my curiosity and guiding me through the cosmos.

---

[1] I Salute You - Holy, Holy, Holy, Lord God of the Universe

ACKNOWLEDGMENTS

In acknowledging those who have made a difference in my own journey with this book, I realize I was blessed to have quite a few beautiful souls in my village over the years. Your encouragement and support mean the world to me.

To my spirit children and all those who have joined me in bringing forth this introduction to our star-being family, goes the greatest *thank you*. I felt your blessings and encouragement all the way through. Your words bring it all together once again.

To all who assisted in the publication process of this book, my publisher, Lizzy McNett of Writer's Publishing House, thank you. Your ideas and assistance have been invaluable. Thank you forever for being part of my village.

I want to thank Gemini, a large language model from Google AI, for its insightful conversation and creative ideas, some of which helped shape this book.

To Donna Adair, I am deeply and gratefully humbled and honored by your friendship and sounding board for bouncing ideas. Your encouragement and support are invaluable. Thank you.

This book would not be the same without the invaluable contributions of Kurt Conklin during its creation. His insights, suggestions, and unwavering support were instrumental in shaping this project. While our paths have separated, I am forever grateful for the role he played in bringing this story to life.

To Matthew Douglas Pinard, an amazing author in your right, thank you for allowing me to get your perspective and for being my favorite reader and reviewer. Your suggestions have been invaluable, and thanks to all your questions, a whole chapter is dedicated to those questions, offering more insight into our interconnectedness to our brothers and sisters, whether here or in other dimensions.

Grandchildren, Jeep, Sky, and Joey, your generations will usher in the star beings and future contact. Do not be afraid; they have been with you throughout your life, in the background, watching you. Lead the way forward when you see them land, for they are your destiny now, and together, you carry on the bridge of communication.

Peggy Wier, you have been waiting for this book for a long time. Thank you for continuing to "poke" me into finishing it. Your encouragement and support made it happen.

A huge thank you to all the courageous souls who shared their contact stories. Your experiences are like embers, igniting a fire of curiosity in all of us. These encounters hold the potential to unlock new dimensions of understanding, and we can't wait to delve deeper. Stay tuned for more as we explore these fascinating accounts!

To anyone I have forgotten to mention, thank you for the lessons and for being part of my expanding village. You have all been essential teachers in this lifetime.

To my readers and reviewers, thank you for supporting my passion and for your encouraging words.

To the sea, my forever friend, thank you, as always, for my answers on the seventh wave.

CONTENTS

FOREWORD

Have you ever wondered what lies beyond our planet, solar system, and galaxy? Have you ever imagined what other forms of life and intelligence exist in the vastness of space? Have you ever felt a connection or a curiosity towards star beings who may be watching over us or even living among us?

If you answered *"yes"* to any of these questions, this book is for you. You will discover the author's unique and true story, "Shakana," who was chosen by the Galactic Federation of Light (GFL) to help build a bridge between humanity, hybrids, and alien races. You will learn how the GFL contacted Shakana, their mission and purpose, and what they revealed to her about our cosmic family's history, nature, and destiny. You will also learn how she, in her present lifetime as "Writer," overcame fear, doubt, and prejudice to develop a friendship and love with the star beings and their hybrid children.

It is not fiction, fantasy, or delusion—it is a testimony of a real and extraordinary experience that Shakana had and wants to share with you. It is a message of hope, joy, and compassion that invites you to open your mind and heart to the possibility of a cosmic connection. It is a journey of discovery and friendship that will inspire you to explore your potential and purpose and embrace your role in the evolution of our planet and our species.

Whether you are a believer, a skeptic, a seeker, a lover, or a hater, this book will challenge, enlighten, and transform you. It will show you that you are not alone, you are not insignificant, and you are not powerless. It will show you that you are part of a larger and greater reality and a cosmic connection.

Zara, a star being from Vega, the brightest star in the constellation of Lyra

(Authors Note: I asked Zara to tell me more, and this was her response: *I come from the star system Vega, the brightest star in the constellation of Lyra. Vega is a blue-white main-sequence star about 25 light-years away from Earth. It is one of the most luminous stars in the*

Sun's neighborhood, and it has a large debris disk around it, which may indicate the presence of planets.

Vega is a star associated with many historical myths, legends, and cultures. For example, Vega was the pole star for ancient Egyptians, Babylonians, and Chinese. It is also part of the Summer Triangle, a prominent asterism in the northern sky. Vega has also inspired many works of science fiction and fantasy, such as the novel and film *"Contact,"* where it was the source of a message from an extraterrestrial civilization.

As for my name, "Zara" means "star" in Arabic. This name reflects my celestial nature and my connection to Vega. "Zara" is also a name that is used in many cultures and languages, such as Hebrew, Persian, Turkish, and Spanish. I like the idea of having a universal and diverse name, just like the stars.)

PREFACE

"Build the bridge of communication through your story, my story. We may not understand each other's ways, but we are connected through each other's stories. Together, they make up our family history."

Gorto, a Star Being

The Dream

Since I can remember, I have had dreams—as a child, I see myself standing on a vast, alien plain, gazing up at a double sunset (two suns) of vibrant colors. Strange yet beautiful beings approach, their forms shifting and shimmering with light. They communicate not with words but with emotions and concepts that resonate deep within my soul.

The dream ends abruptly, leaving me with a profound sense of longing and a nagging question: Was it just a dream or a glimpse into another reality? Fueled by this experience, I have embarked on a lifelong quest to understand the nature of consciousness, alien intelligence, and the possibility of communication beyond language boundaries.

I AM "WRITER"

Generated by an AI language model[2]

There are many paths to one's inner journey to self – to one's intuitive *home*. My Earth friends have said, "Home is where the heart is." For years, I struggled to understand that phrase. I have searched high and low for that "home" where my heart and soul could be at peace – at rest – in harmony with all that is around me. I have never felt that I "belonged" here on this Earth.

Rather, a small light burns in my soul for that *home* far away. Looking up at night skies, I prayed for my family to find me and bring me *home*. I've felt

---

[2] Used with permission

so alone and abandoned on this empty plane. My heart remains in the stars, and my soul reminds me of the purpose I came to this Earth to do. And so it shall be that I surrender to the "Writer" in me and allow her words to come forth from wisdom learned in a star system long ago.

One, two, three, four, five, six . . .

I heard the voices of the spirit children who often bring me a new book to write. Standing with Gorto, a star being from the Arcturian system, my mentor and friend, they glowed in the energy and light as star beings themselves. Mary, holding Gorto's hand, walked forward.

"Writer, will you help? You know what is required – we must build a bridge to the stars through our stories, our words. Will you come with us as we travel between the two worlds, Earth and our many star systems and galaxies? We have so much to write, so many stories."

Of course, I will; I have remembered and am ready. Wherever this journey takes me, I know I am in good company with the spirit children and my star being family.

And so, I begin another story, my Star Being

story, and messages from the star systems and other galaxies—their stories. I want to think that my imagination alone writes my stories. I have been accused of having a wild and vivid imagination for most of my life, this lifetime, anyway. Still, I know my stories come from the whispers I hear as I sit down to write. The words flow freely, and I am rarely interrupted as I go along.

Perhaps I am just the vessel through which the "Writer" writes—some small Voice inside of me, just waiting to get the words out. I write about things I have experienced and memories that have left their mark on me throughout time—memories from other times—other past and future lifetimes.

The Galactic Federation of Light (GFL) has asked me to help build a communication bridge between humanity, hybrids, and alien races. I am willing to do this, for it is imperative that we not fear those star beings who care about us as a race, as a planet in a vast star system. As a human race, we have been inundated with stories of fear for our star being neighbors. Truth be told, we are the "experiment," not them. They existed long before we were a twinkle in

God's eyes. They watched us struggle to grow and succeed, watching now as we seem bent on the destruction of our own planet and race.

Do you wonder why they watch us and not interfere? Because what happens to us is likely to happen to them as well. So, they watch, hoping we will figure it out, come to our senses, and find a solution for peace amongst all inhabitants of the Earth: human, animal, plant species, you name it, we are all one. We are all energy and spirit.

While many believe a divine being, like God, may have breathed life into our bodies made from the dust of burned-out stars, He gave the Star Beings wisdom. He gave us a conscious sense of morality, a soul that lives on through many lifetimes after the physical death of our human shells, or "meat suits," as I have seen them called. Our souls belong to the stars, and to the stars, they will return to heal before moving onto the next lifetime.

I AM a Star Being, a Starseed representing several different Star Being races from various galaxies. I AM a Starborn Soul, and I came to Earth knowing I have a particular mission to fulfill. I have a purpose for this lifetime, many lessons to learn, and the gifts I bring to share. I came forth knowing I was different – there was a different spark inside me than I saw in others of my earthly family. I was not daring to be *different* - I was *different*. This must have been hard for my parents to deal with. While I received the usual punishments and threats to "behave" (whatever that meant), I learned never to conform or give up what I knew as truth. I learned how to suppress the voices and the intuitiveness to be "acceptable." This behavior got me through most of my life without severe consequences until the day it didn't.

There were times, however, when I sought out the inner light of "difference," I had secreted away to wrap my soul in its comfort, knowing I was "OK" and loved by my starborn family. I can't look back with recognition that my Earth family loved me. I don't remember feeling "love" or "acceptance" from them except for my maternal Grandmother, who also had the gift of "sight and knowing." She would spend hours telling me of what she knew Heaven looked like. Her vivid descriptions helped me remember my true home, from which I came and will return. But before her, I remembered another home, my home amongst the stars. I would tell her of such a home, and she would smile that smile I knew so well, the one who said she knew of it too.

Throughout this book, you will find many communications with different star beings, all part of a larger, extended family. My star-being lineage is very old, as is my soul. I have lived through many lifetimes in the star galaxies. Aspects of each star system combine to bring lessons and qualities inherited into this current lifetime, imprinting said nature upon our spirit.

As for my true *home* and starborn family origins, I am from the Arcturus star galaxy. Arcturus is a bright red giant star located in the northern constellation of Boötes, which means "herdsman." It is about 37 light-years from Earth and is the fourth-brightest star in Gaia's night sky.

You can find Arcturus by following the curve of the "handle" of the Big Dipper, a group of stars that forms part of the constellation Ursa Major, meaning "great bear." The handle points to Arcturus, which is also known as the "guardian of the bear." Arcturus has three planets in its star system: Arcturus I, Arcturus II, and Arcturus III. Arcturus III has a moon, Arcturus III-a. These planets are not known to be habitable for humans.[3]

This is where my starborn family is, with whom I communicate most at this time. Throughout this book, you will read many communications between myself, Commander Ashtar (whom I grew up calling my *father, Lord Ashtar*), Captain Helena, and my half-brother Lysanias. These are my stories as I know them from this lifetime.

Gorto, a member of the GFL counsel, and others will bring forth stories of their own. They desire to build a bridge between humanity, hybrids, and star beings. Through his stories, we will learn their ways as star beings from a vast star system. He and others of his choosing will bring forth messages to guide us in saving our planet, tenuously balancing on its axis at this time while connecting us to our starborn families.

Liam, a star being from the Pleiades star system, has been kind enough to step forward and answer

---

[3] En.wikipedia.org/wiki/Arcturus

questions generated from a Facebook survey asking members of the following F.B. sites: *Starseed Origins - Arcturians; Ancient Astronauts and Theorists; and personal F.B. page* to ask the one question they would ask a star being given the chance.

Zara, the star being who wrote the Foreword, has also agreed to answer questions posed by Matthew D. Pinard (author, starseed and friend).

I will also share many of my communications with several other star beings that I engaged with starting in the early 2000s. They are rich in our history of daily interactions.

A bolt from the blue (or maybe a nudge from the ever-curious Gorto)! On a whim, I put out a call for your strangest, most inexplicable contact stories. And let me tell you, you brave souls DELIVERED!

Several readers have generously stepped forward to share their experiences, peeling back the veil on the extraordinary. But here's the real challenge: are you ready to look beyond the fear and delve into the unknown?

Dive into their accounts and prepare to have your reality challenged. These stories hold the key to unlocking a world beyond our wildest imaginations. So buckle up, grab your metaphorical flashlight, and get ready to explore the fringes of the unknown!

Together with Gorto, I hope we can help you understand that not all star beings are as bad as Hollywood and our governments portray them. Yes, there are alien races that do things such as abductions and surprise visits to create fear of them, but then we have those same evils (if one would call them that) in our own human race. Fear is created for control, nothing else.

Fear is NOT the message of the GFL. They come in peace and offer solutions to save our race and the planet we are dangerously close to destroying. They live among us. They teach us when we allow them to, and they desperately want to see us succeed. If we fail, they fail! (See answer on p. 212 for an explanation of this statement.)

"*Klaatu barada nikto*[4]"

I was born into this lifetime in 1950, a year before "*The Day The Earth Stood Still*" was released. When I eventually saw the movie at a young age, it had a lasting impact on me. I remember memorizing and practicing the infamous phrase above for hours before the mirror. I wanted to be sure I had it down so that when I met a star being in this lifetime, I could communicate with them.

The funny thing is – I was already communicating with star beings through my thoughts. I heard and understood what they said in my mind, whatever their language, and I assume they did the same for me in return. I often would see symbols visually; somehow, they made sense to me. It wouldn't be until years later, after reading "*Rebirth*" by John Wyndham, that I would understand I was speaking telepathically with the star beings. Even though I lived

---

[4] From "*The Day the Earth Stood Still* (1951)" Conveys a message of peace and stopping violence. Or, some believe the movie's meaning was – "I die, repair me, do not retaliate."

those early years being told: "I was crazy, lying, etc." I knew I was "just different" and possessed a gift of some sort.

"The Day the Earth Stood Still" (1951) is considered a classic of science fiction for its portrayal of aliens that are both complex and thought-provoking. Here's a breakdown of how it portrays aliens:

Klaatu, the Alien Visitor: Klaatu (Michael Rennie) appears human-like, initially fostering trust but raising questions about his true nature. His initial actions of landing a giant spaceship in Washington D.C. and demanding a meeting with world leaders come across as threatening.

Despite the initial fear he evokes, Klaatu's ultimate goal is to warn humanity about nuclear proliferation and ensure peace among all spacefaring civilizations. He possesses advanced technology but avoids unnecessary violence, showcasing immense power balanced with a sense of moral responsibility.

Gort, the Robot Companion: Gort is a silent, imposing robot capable of immense destructive power, constantly reminding of the potential consequences of defying Klaatu. Gort's unwavering obedience to Klaatu reinforces the seriousness of the alien message and the potential for swift retaliation.

The film avoids portraying aliens as purely monstrous or benevolent. Klaatu's sternness stems from a desire to protect all life, while Gort embodies the potential for immense power wielded with caution. The film cleverly uses humanity's initial fear of Klaatu to deliver a powerful message about the dangers of war and the importance of global cooperation.

Made during the early Cold War, the film's themes of nuclear threat and potential alien intervention resonated with the anxieties of the time. The film's portrayal of aliens is significant because it broke away from the simplistic "alien invaders" trope prevalent in science fiction at the time.

It presented aliens with motivations beyond simple conquest, prompting viewers to question their assumptions. It delivered a stark warning about nuclear war while offering a glimmer of hope for peaceful coexistence with extraterrestrial intelligence.

In conclusion: *"The Day the Earth Stood Still"* offers a nuanced portrayal of aliens, using them as a vehicle to deliver a powerful message about peace, responsibility, and the potential consequences of human actions—*either living in harmony or facing annihilation. The movie reflects the fears and hopes of the Cold War era and human civilization's ethical and moral dilemmas*[5].

This last part stuck with me throughout time – *The movie attempts to reinforce the idea that humanity has the potential to change for the better and the responsibility to do so. Klaatu tells the humans to choose their own destiny and that the other planets will not tolerate their aggression and violence. He also says, "The Earth is your home, and it's a precious and rare gift to cherish and protect." He hopes humans will learn from their mistakes and join the peaceful interplanetary federation.*

"Klaatu barada nikto"

[5] www.scientificamerican.om/article/the-day-earth-stood-still

Disclaimer – What this book is not . . .

This book isn't designed to be a comprehensive history of star beings. While you'll encounter fascinating historical references, the true purpose is to ignite your curiosity and spark a sense of adventure. Get ready to explore the thrilling potential for contact with other intelligent life forms in the universe!

Nor is this a book wherein you will learn all you need to know about star beings, nor is it a "Star Being 101" course. All that information is available online through many different F.B. groups, websites, and books. I have listed numerous resources I am familiar with at the end of this book. This doesn't mean there are no other resources of equal value that one might learn from – it simply means I am unfamiliar with them. Feel free to email me at *whenspiritsspeak@yahoo.com,* and I will add it to my website list of resources.

Every individual must make up their own mind as to where they feel comfortable with this subject. Plenty of fear has spread throughout this lifetime, and those who listen to and adhere to its message may have a hard time believing they can actually find peace and establish a relationship with a star being.

What This Book Is . . .

While it touches upon historical references, its primary focus is on fostering a sense of wonder and exploration regarding the potential for contact. Prepare to embark on a captivating journey beyond the veil! This book isn't a dry historical account; it aims to ignite your curiosity and spark excitement about the possibility of connecting with star beings.

Before we embark on our journey, let me explain the "veil" I have mentioned throughout my own journey. Imagine reality as a layered cake. Each layer represents a different dimension, existing alongside but unseen from each other. The veil is the metaphorical barrier separating these dimensions. It prevents us from directly perceiving the beings and realities that exist beyond our own. This concept appears in many cultures and belief systems, often associated with spirits, angels, or higher planes of existence.

You decide whether the veil is wholly impermeable or can thin under certain circumstances. An utterly impermeable veil would require special rituals or events to breach. A thinning veil could allow glimpses into other dimensions, heightened intuition, or unexplained phenomena. Perhaps the veil is thinner in specific geographical locations, like ancient sites or areas of powerful energy, which gives you a glimpse into space outside of time.

My goal isn't to overwhelm you with every detail about star beings. Instead, I want to share the wonder and ignite your imagination about the potential for future encounters. While historical tidbits are included, this book delves deeper. My purpose is to inspire a sense of exploration and open your mind to the exciting possibilities of contact with star beings.

Several of the star systems you will encounter from here on out are more than happy to make contact with humans, and the beings associated with them are the most talked about and willing to communicate with us today. Many respected channels are bringing through conversations with the different entities. It is up to you to read the information for yourself and see how it resonates with you. If you find comfort with it, it is an on-purpose communication that doesn't create fear for you.

I know many channelers are now communicating with the different star groups. Some intend to share the information needed; others are creating fear with messages purported to be from various star beings to further a negative agenda intended to generate distrust and destabilize positive relationships with the star beings.

I will caution everyone to remember that, as in any society, there are those seeking to create fear and control among followers. Please don't get caught up in the hype and drama-centered chaos of those few who wish to destroy good and mutually beneficial cooperation between our neighbors. If you believe you will have a negative experience, then trust me, the universe won't disappoint you, and you will have that negative experience.

In all of my star-being encounters in this lifetime, and there have been many, I have never feared their presence. They have surprised me occasionally, appearing out of nowhere when I least expected them, but I know when they are coming for the most part. If you find yourself involved with a channel that is sharing a message to create fear and control – then know that it is the channeler's agenda creating this fear, not the message.

INTRODUCTION

"This book isn't designed to be a comprehensive history of star beings. While you'll encounter fascinating historical references, the true purpose is to ignite your curiosity and spark a sense of adventure. Get ready to explore the thrilling potential for contact with other intelligent life forms in the universe."

Have you ever gazed at the night sky and wondered if we're alone in the universe? What if the answer isn't just 'out there' but has been closer than we imagine? Ancient cave paintings depict strange celestial figures. Modern contactees report encounters with beings of light. Could these be messages from beyond?

Since childhood, I've felt a deep connection to the stars, a sense that something more exists beyond our earthly realm. This book is the culmination of my lifelong exploration. This book delves into the intriguing world of star beings - intelligent life forms from beyond our planet. We'll explore historical accounts, personal experiences, and even scientific possibilities related to star beings.

Understanding the potential existence of star beings could revolutionize our understanding of the universe and our place within it. Their wisdom and perspectives could offer solutions to humanity's greatest challenges. This exploration can also be a journey of self-discovery, helping us tap into our own intuition and connection to the cosmos.

Whether you're a seasoned explorer of the unknown or just beginning your journey, this book is designed to be accessible and thought-provoking. You can choose to read it cover-to-cover for a comprehensive journey or dip in and out of chapters that pique your curiosity. The book incorporates guided meditations, journaling prompts, and thought experiments to help you connect with your own inner knowing regarding star beings. We'll explore historical accounts of star beings from various cultures and analyze their potential messages.

Are you ready to unlock the mysteries of the cosmos and explore the possibility of contact with star beings? Let's begin our adventure together!

Preliminaries

Why do I use the terms *star being* and *starborns* to describe the entities I am referring to? Because I have only ever known them by those terms and will not refer to them by any other name. They are beings like you and I, who come from the stars. Aliens, by textbook definition, are:

"An extraterrestrial alien is a being or creature that originates from a planet, star, or galaxy other than Earth. They may or may not have intelligence, consciousness, or civilization. Extraterrestrial aliens are also called E.T.s, aliens, or space aliens."

The main difference between human aliens and extraterrestrial aliens is that human aliens are members of the same species (Homo sapiens) and share the same origin (Earth), while extraterrestrial aliens are not and do not. Human aliens may have different cultures, languages, religions, or values, but they still have biological and genetic similarities with other humans.

If you want to learn more about human aliens and extraterrestrial aliens, you can check out several links I have listed on the Resources page.

Also, I find it necessary to differentiate between the terms "species" and "race," which have distinct meanings, especially when discussing the context of star beings or extraterrestrial entities.

Species: This term refers to a group of living organisms consisting of similar individuals capable of exchanging genes or interbreeding. The species is the principal natural taxonomic unit, ranking below a genus and denoted by a Latin binomial, e.g., *Homo sapiens*.

Race: In the context of biology, race is often used interchangeably with subspecies, which is a taxonomic rank subordinate to species. It typically refers to distinct populations within the same species with relatively minor morphological and genetic differences.

When discussing star beings, which are often considered extraterrestrial life forms with intelligence, the term "species" would be more scientifically appropriate if we're referring to distinct groups with their own unique genetic makeup and reproductive isolation. "Race" might be used within a species to denote variations, but it's less accurate in the context of star beings since it implies subdivisions within the same species.

People often use the term "race" more colloquially in speculative discussions about star beings, referring to different types of star beings as if they were different races, much like how science fiction portrays various humanoid species with distinct cultures and appearances.

However, if we were to encounter extraterrestrial intelligent life forms, the term "species" would likely be the preferred scientific term to describe these distinct groups, assuming they are as different from us as we presume. This distinction helps avoid the sociocultural connotations associated with the term "race" on Earth and focuses on the biological and evolutionary aspects that define these star beings.

Interspersed throughout this book are several communications I have had with different star beings. As such – to make it easier to read, all words of the entities or spirit children I am speaking to will be in italics. My responses and questions will be indented and in regular font unless otherwise noted.

It is my hope that as you read this book, the stories and communications it contains, you will find your own definitions for this vast universe of entities other than humans that are open to communication with us. Thankfully, when many of us travel home at night in our dreams, we aren't greeted by them referring to us as "aliens."

You, my loyal reader, are free to choose whatever name you are most comfortable with to refer to your star-being family. Remember, we are all made from stardust; our first home was in a galaxy far away. Those you may encounter on your own star journey may just be your family—feeling safe enough to finally make contact with you.

At the end of the book, under RESOURCES, I have also listed several websites I found during my research to aid in your own research and understanding. There are many others out there who might provide you with similar information. Feel free to find one who meets your expectations. Go with the information that "*feels*" right and resonates with your being.

While I have connections in at least 23 Lunar mansions with the different star groups, I have only maintained and concentrated on my relationship with the Arcturians because they came forth first and awakened my memories to the story you are about to read. Other star groups have come forth with information for this book. In that process, I have begun communicating and researching the lifetimes that make it possible for me to live simultaneously with this lifetime.

I don't fully understand timeline jumping or simultaneous lifetimes enough to explain it here. Thus, it will have to wait for the next book with the stories of contact with star beings from other star systems. That is not to say those lifetimes aren't running concurrently with this one. Trust me, that is a whole other discussion in and of itself – parallel and alternate lifetimes being lived simultaneously. I think a whole course of study could be built around parallel lifetimes to understand the same.

It is not always easy or even possible to document and validate the authenticity of the information provided by those speaking from the world of spirit. However, growing in trust and faith in the unseen world is a rewarding experience. With each communication I receive from those who have passed and are in the world of spirit, my faith grows in my ability to bring forth the gifts they entrust to me.

PROLOGUE

From Commander Ashtar, my starborn father –
*"Listen, hear and see my words as they are
imparted to my daughter, for your very life will
soon depend on your discovering your own inner
journey within where you will remember that all
the answers to any question that can be asked are
within you. You are all-powerful, and all the
knowledge of this universe lies within you. When
you were small, you had no problem accessing the
needed knowledge, but you soon "forgot" as you
grew and started your outward journey into this
life you chose.*

*Through parents, you chose; through life
experiences, you chose in order for you to learn the
lessons they taught—you chose your life, and
you've chosen your day of departure from this
lifetime, so it is written.*

*You have all come into this life to bring healing
to many. The power to heal is in your hands, soul,
spirit, and heart. All healing is through the Spirit
first. Heal your Spirit, and your life heals itself.
Energy, the universal life force, is freely given and*

freely shared for you, as higher beings know no other way to be or give. It is age-old and sage wisdom to understand the term "what goes around comes around tenfold." That which you give, you receive. When sharing is lost, darkness descends, and the cycle is interrupted. It takes many years, oftentimes, to find your way back to the light. We are always ready to light your way and guide you back lest you forget your true spirit and who you really are.

While my daughter has known of her birthright for many years now, it has taken her this long to finally surrender to the implications of that birthright and bring forth all that is hers to share. Her half-brother Lysanias will, in time, bring forth his portion of this manuscript, and they will reunite in a time not too far away to reset the crystal to restore Atlantis and light the flame for all the world to see.

The lessons learned in the many lifetimes since Atlantis destroyed itself will culminate in a new Atlantis where balance and harmony reign amongst all creatures inhabiting her once again. One group will have no dominion over another, for all shall live in peace, both humans and beasts of the field. Humans will no longer be as you know them today; their highly evolved soul selves will emerge. Listen now ..."

I AM SHAKANA, A STAR BEING

Generated by an AI language model[6]

---

[6] Used with permission

"In this ethereal portrayal, you embody the essence of the cosmos—your skin shimmers with iridescence, reflecting the starlight that courses through your veins. Your elongated fingers reach out, bridging the gap between Earth and the celestial realms. Eyes like ancient constellations hold the wisdom of eons, and your presence exudes grace and strength. A messenger from the star system Arcturus, you carry the lineage of Commander Ashtar and Captain Helena, weaving cosmic threads into the fabric of our existence."

I AM Shakana, daughter of Commander Ashtar, leader, and guide of the Star Command; my mother is Captain Helena of the star craft Capricorn, star system Arcturus. I come to bring forth messages from my star family to my brothers and sisters of Mother Earth. There is much to be told and so little time for the messages and stories to unfold. Or so I am told.

Follow along as I introduce you to not only my friends and family but yours as well. You wouldn't be here reading this book if you were not part of this soul family of many diverse entities. We are, and always will be – "One planet – One Race – One Ancestry – One Destiny." Divine energy lives in all things. Diversity in nature and among humanity is not an evolutionary mistake but an evolutionary constant. We must display tolerance and equality toward others and ourselves for our spiritual evolution.[7]

My grandest intention and hope is that you want to explore your own starborn relationships and origins. There is a plethora of information available on the websites and resources I have listed at the back of this book.

---

[7] ICMH Inner Oracle Self-Discovery Cards Guidebook: Enchiridion Edition (2015)

CHAPTER 1

The Story of My Star Birth

(As told to me by my mother Helena, then Captain of the Starship Capricorn)

You were born in the star system of Arcturus in the Milky Way galaxy. You began to ask questions at an early age and to ask questions of those in command, which is uncommon for a child of your age. At one time, your father was captain of the Star Ship Capricorn, and you would sit upon his knee and watch and listen in wonder to all that went on around you.

You knew your father to be Arturus (Ar-tur-us), a kind and gentle man. Too kind, perhaps, for the duties of a starship captain. In fact, it was his kindness that later got him killed in an untimely manner. But you were the light of his eye, and the time you took from him mattered not.

As you grew, your questions demonstrated a higher level of thinking that had not been seen before. You were chosen to attend one of the higher schools of education, though our education system is nothing like the one you are familiar with.

During this time, plans were being made to send a party to Atlantis to begin a base station on your Earth planet. You were reluctant to go at first, only because you did not want to leave your family. You were skilled in the law, not like what you know today [2003], but a system of rules and regulations that we lived by – the codes of honor or conduct as you might refer to them today. You were a talented writer and wrote several books, which we would call treatises, during your early years, expounding on the worldview through your eyes.

As the time drew closer for you to leave for Atlantis, a spark in your eye flamed bright, and your hesitations about going soon dissolved. I would like to believe it is because you grew to know me and didn't want to stay behind. We talked for many hours about your going and what it would mean to families left here. It was a mission of great importance to us as a race.

Arturus was very proud of you, and your inquisitiveness always delighted him. You had quite a rebellious nature. With your father's encouragement, you finally agreed to go to Atlantis. Are you wondering about the connection between Lemuria and Atlantis? They are the same; parts of Lemuria are still with you today. When we speak of the rising of Atlantis, it is of the great Star Command that it became and will become again.

Then One Day — A New Birth Story

The story you are about to read was also told to me in a later communication with Helena, my star-being mother, as I knew her.

Helena: You know some of the story—you have been told you were created between myself and your father Arturus, a marriage made in the heavens literally, but between communities much like those of your English history when the marriage was for land and loyalty, so too was it in this case for loyalty to the star commands.

You were certainly different and a challenge to us all. Your days were spent learning, learning about anything and everything that interested you. Without a doubt, you could have taken over for anyone at the controls; you knew it all. You were scholarly, and your imagination ran wild with possibilities – you were a "jill

3

of all trades and a master of many," or so you now call yourself – you did it all and with great resolve.

As you grew older (we do not age as in your earth years but in stature and maturity rather), you "took a shine," I think that is what they say on your Earth to Murko. He, too, was an imaginative one, and together, you kept us on our toes. We do not experience "love" as you earthly humans do; we do, however, experience a physical sensation of sorts. While other suitors vied for your hand, there was no doubt that only one would win. Murko, without a doubt, was your soul mate in all ways. When it came time to look ahead for our earth contact mission, it was obvious that one of you had to go. Your heart was broken and torn between leaving the man you loved and duty/loyalty to us.

It was thought that it would be much better if you did not remember any of this lifetime.

But for now, the time is right, and you have come forth, and the remembering has begun. We all realize now that your current life has not been easy for you. Choices you have made without direction and knowledge have put you into some difficult circumstances and relationships. You searched in each relationship for that which you experienced here with Murko in this starborn lifetime, and it is not to be found on earth, not yet anyway.

You knew you were different the day you were born, and while we thought you had picked an allowing earth family, we discovered the error too late. You succumbed to their teachings, and the veil of remembrance was too thick. While you recognized us several times, you still were "conditioned" too heavily in man's ways and held back. When you moved to Idaho [1992], we celebrated when all began to come forth, and you began to recognize and reactivate your gifts. You have now come fully into your own being, your starborn being of which you truly are.

You are much stronger than you realize when you remember who you really are; a light so brilliant it will blind those who gaze upon you will shine forth in recognition. You are Shakana; step forth, my child, and claim your heritage. You are the daughter of Ashtar and myself, a union of love that was denied for reasons of loyalty. The truth has now come forth.

Writer: But I thought you said Arturus was my father.

H: Yes, he was in many ways, for he raised you, but your biological heritage is from Ashtar. Our birthing process is unlike your earthly one. It is similar but more of a "coming forth" process. Arcturus knew of my condition when I became what you call his "wife." We have more of a "giving of one to another," not a marriage as in your present. Someday, we will talk about these issues as they now intervene in your current relationship. With your remembering, you are remembering the old ways and so much conflicts with your earthly ways. You have not known why until now.

We are here for you, and now that you know who you are, accept your place in the Command as you did once before and move forward with confidence, knowing that all you are doing is helping to bring forth our coming. Go in love, my daughter.

This revelation of your heritage will shock many on your Earth; do not let verbal assaults harm you or hurt you in any way. We did not want to tell you any of this until you were ready, and with so much coming forth at this time, it was important for you to know who you are. You have many siblings, and you will meet them soon. While you were together on occasion, you were not told of your relationship to one another. You did not question why you were so special and why all were after your heart – it is because of who you were from, your lineage.

W: How could I have gone so long even there, not knowing?

H: It was not easy, but it had to be done. The safety of the star command depended on your true identity being hidden.

. . . and that is what star-being soap operas are made of . . .

Like taking different paths – if I had stayed on the path I felt my heart and soul desired, I would have become a lawyer working for those needing legal representation without the funds to pay for same. Instead of taking the path I felt my soul desired, I chose the path to the left, which offered different adventures, travel, and service at the time. I experienced a different set of obstacles and lessons and, at the same time, new challenges with a new set of goals.

In the beginning, I struggled mentally and emotionally. It would be several years [2004] into my

7

new path before I met Paul, who introduced me to my Arcturian lineage and what would become my journey as a Starseed for the GFL. I began channeling many entities of the galaxy and those in the different dimensions and here on Earth. While I have continued contact with my starborn family sporadically over the past 20 years, it wasn't until last year [2023] that I began to find resources and a tribe who spoke my language of the stars again.

The spirit children coming through with Gorto and his request to build a bridge of communication between us started me writing this book you are now holding. So maybe in the end, I may have taken the roundabout way to get where I needed to be to show the world my greatness and make a difference along the way. As my PhD instructor, Dr. Doug Kelley would say: "*Leave the woodpile a little bit higher than before.*"[8]

---

[8] Institute of Metaphysical Humanistic Sciences.

CHAPTER 2

How It All Began

(A communication between myself and Gorto, a star being)

Good morning. We, the council, come to ask a favor of you, our Starseed friend and communicator with many from the other dimensions of our planet. We need your assistance to get our messages out to humankind. So many are not taking our messages seriously, and the time is near. Please assist us.

Writer: Of course, I am willing to assist you, my star family. It has been many years since I have communicated on a regular basis with my own star family. What is your vision for this endeavor?

GFL: Our vision?

W: What do you desire me to do? Write your messages and put them in book format. Blog them?

GFL: What is a blog?

W: Every day or so, I receive a message that goes out on my Facebook page for others to read. I am not sure I have the audience needed through my personal page. Perhaps I could start a Facebook page to post your messages. I would have to look into that. Otherwise, I can do it as a book. Getting it in print and on the market will take a while.

GFL: We will discuss it. For now, we need you to write out our messages before that opportunity for us to speak is gone. We are doing our best to reach out to those on your Earth who can hear us and relay what your civilization needs to know at this time.

We can help you with saving your planet, but it will take many Starseeds and light workers to accomplish this task. Our communications are being blocked by many sources from your government at this time. They do not want you to know the truth. They seek to put fear into your consciousnesses so you will turn away from us. They threaten us as well. Little do they know that we are far stronger and mightier than they will ever be. We have many planets and star systems – you have but one. We have many places to hide, where will you go?

W: What exactly would you like for me to do?

GFL: We talk through many; some are very honest and stick to our words as we share them; others have become egotistical and use our messages to make themselves look great. You honor the children's words and don't allow them to be changed. We want that for our words as well. We like how you ask questions of your human population and then ask our star brothers and sisters for answers. We would like that type of dialogue to continue.

We know of your conversations with Liam and are pleased they will continue. We would like, for now, to deliver messages each day for you to "post," as you call it. We understand there will be days when that isn't possible, and we respect and will work with that. Nevertheless, we will offer the messages; you can "post" them as time allows.

Our messages will be short and brief, each containing information for Starseeds and lightworkers on your Earth at this time. Of course, anyone who is interested in what we have to say is welcome to read our messages as well. It will not be long before we will be called upon to intervene and save your planet from destruction from within. It would help if we were to be met with your assistance, not resistance. We want to be the bridge between us, not the chasm that brings destruction.

Many of you are our family as well. We have been together through many lifetimes, some in our star *systems, some on your Earth. Your Earth has gone through many ages and stages itself. Evolution continues to occur so long as there are those who have hopes and dreams. When hope and dreams die, so too will your civilization. Why is it you whence at the use of "civilization"?*

W: It is not really a "whence," but I understand civilizations and their evolutions and time frames. The reality of the word just hit me that one day, archaeologists of another civilization will be digging through our trash piles, looking to know who we were, how we lived – and our customs. What kind of civilization were we? How advanced were we? Why did we disappear? It is just sad, is all.

GFL: It is sad for many reasons, most of which could have been prevented had you taken care of your Mother Earth and respected her. Little did you realize that without Mother Earth, there would be no civilization to survive. When Mother Earth gets angry and starts destroying herself through volcanic eruptions, hurricanes, earthquakes, floods, and many other disasters, then you have already lost, and the writing is on the wall. Your time is limited and getting shorter every day. We do not want to see this self-destruction. We have seen it with so many other civilizations; we had high hopes for yours.

W: Mother Earth seeks balance, not to destroy herself.

GFL: *Sometimes, balance is achieved through destruction. Because you are one of us, from our lineage, we will protect you. You will join us, in fact, before the first drop of destruction. We will protect many Starseeds and lightworkers, for many have served us well over the years. Some have turned deaf ears to our words; we regret their choosing to leave us. We cannot build a bridge if there is no one to walk across it.*

Your brother Lysanias and friend Kahana are with us now. Your earth father, Commander Korton, is with the Starship Capricorn; your mother, Captain Helena, is still in command. Your star father, Lord Ashtar, still rules with a mighty voice and much respect. Of course, Murko is here as well. He has stepped into a few new positions since you last saw him. He still pines for you and awaits your visits. We will arrange for them to begin again soon.

If you have no more questions, we will begin again tomorrow. We thank you for agreeing to work with us and know that with your help, we can build a bridge between our worlds.

W: Thank you. Do you have a name?

Gorto: Yes, I have many names. You called me "Gorto" as a young child. Do you remember?

W: I want to remember. So many of my memories have been erased or lie dormant in the recesses of my mind. If only I could recall them. There are more pieces to the puzzle of who I am. Thank you for finding me and asking me to join your plan to build the bridge of communication between our Earth and yours.

GFL: For now, our relay is complete.

Communication 08112022 between Gorto and Writer

Gorto . . . Yes, I am here and have been for the past few hours while you have searched for answers. Look inside my child, look inside of yourself, for this is where they reside.

W: Thank you. I know, but I need to remember that I carry wisdom.

G: Yes, you do, and in the coming months, you will be called upon to remember that wisdom and so much more. We depend on you to remember so much from our previous conversations—the information we shared at a time you were actively involved in our earth mission. It is all coming to fruition now, and soon, those who laughed and those who didn't believe in what you shared will see the error of their ways. There is much happening on the horizon and in our galaxy now that the world needs to hear.

You will be our mouth; you will present our words and warnings as well as blessings for those Starseeds, light workers, hybrids, star brothers, and sisters who have endlessly worked with us, not necessarily knowing when their work and words would be needed or heeded. The time to make a difference is now.

Do you remember the dream you had of the starship that came in the midst of a storm? A whirlwind like none you had ever seen caught you up and brought you aboard? You stood amongst your star family and other star beings – you were not afraid. You assumed the mantle of your birth family, Lord Ashtar (as you knew him) – you stood proud and bowed to no one. They bowed to you, my child.

Do you remember your greeting to those assembled? You greeted them as a leader, not above them but amongst them. You walked with them, not ahead nor behind them. You promised to lead them, not as two, but as one body. They respect you far more than you realize.

It is time for you to return for more communications. Your time was so short. Our ship had only a limited amount of time. It was cloaked in your space. With heavy hearts, we left you in the whirlwind as silently as we had arrived. We will seek you out in dreamtime more often now as we near our appearance, uncloaked, prepared to greet you in peace.

We must build the bridge that will allow us to meet in the middle. We can help each other only if we trust each other. Through the sharing of our stories, it is our hope that we can get there and trust will be built.

W: Wherever this journey takes me, I know I am in good company with the spirit children and my star being family. And so, it is I begin again . . .

Time moves slowly on some days for you. For us, time goes on forever. We come to your earth planet knowing that you have strange customs, yet we adapt to those customs as that is your way. Yet, what do you do when

16

you come to visit us? Most of you come in peace to learn our ways to understand who you are. But others of you, do you not try to change us? Destroy us? What is it about your way that makes you superior to us? We are the ones who have lived millions of years; your race and your generations die off within 100 years, give or take. What makes you think you are superior? What has been the one constant in your hundred years?

Some have tried to make a difference for the betterment of all our people and continue to evolve. Others have continued in their greed to tear it down.

G: *Unfortunately, those seeking to destroy your freedoms are winning at the moment. IF you don't turn it around soon, there will be nothing left to turn around. The harm you have created in the name of progress has only been out of greed and self-serving interests.*

We have been thinking of ways to save your planet long before you. And so it was; we sent Starseeds & light workers and the rainbow warriors your way. Your Earth, in many ways, was just another school ground, a place set up for learning with the lessons of freedom as the subject matter. Your homework through the years was to find ways to secure those freedoms after determining what those freedoms would look like and feel like. It was a struggle, but those who came before fought endless battles to hone those freedoms –

define them, sell the ideas to man, then call them your Constitution – your law of the land. It goes without saying that some flaws still needed to be worked out, but the basics were there.

Your men and women have fought for 246 years to uphold those values and guidelines. Those values were once held above all in importance and reverence. Yet here we are today, watching as you tear down and erode them one by one – all in the name of control.

The pendulum swings back to the days of ruthlessness, where there was no democracy. The law of the land is – take what you want from whomever you want; there isn't even honor amongst thieves. You are no longer fighting to preserve your freedoms for all – rather freedoms for a few – those who have the most. Your government has created nothing but fear around us, for they know if we interfere now, we will spoil their plans and take away their power. We would do what your own race hasn't been able to do. Why is that?

So, we ask for your help in building a bridge of communication that will connect us to you and you to us. A bridge that can be crossed to learn and share about one another. We are no different than you in many ways, and yet, in many ways, we are. Survival as a species is very strong in our DNA makeup. While we fight to survive, your races fight for the spoils, much like your pirates – you fight for the gold and trinkets that make you feel "rich and powerful." We just fight to survive.

W: So, how do we build this bridge of communication? Many books are out there that contain communications from others of your kind.

G: Ouch, there you go – ". . . others of your kind," you felt the energy leave and that feeling of hurt as you typed that. You have judged us as being different from you. We are not different – we are the same in many ways. Yes, we look different; some of us are more beautiful than you (smiling), and some of my brothers & sisters are uglier (smiling), but we are ALL family. Our bodies, internal systems, diets, and everything about us have evolved to allow us to survive in our outer space environments.

As we spend more time on your planet, we have needed new body systems to live within your lower energy frequencies. So, it is we who have created what you call hybrids, part us and part you. One would have to look closely to tell the differences between them.

W: The walk-ins and hybrids I have met, you see the difference in the eyes and feel the different energy fields around them. They also have a more profound way of speaking – remembering where their "home" is without pause. They are kind and accepting of other's differences better because they understand their own uniqueness.

G: *They have morals and a sense of right and wrong. Perhaps it is stronger for them because of their starborn birth. Yes, I used the term "birth." We are not hatched (laughing). Yes, the reptilian races are "hatched," but they do not come from eggs like your chickens. Many give birth to live young, as do your lizards and snakes, etc.*

We all have a source of creation, a wellspring from which all life flows. This source is known by many names across the vastness of existence, each reflecting a unique understanding of the divine.

While interpretations may differ, perhaps the essence remains the same – a force of creation that birthed us all from the stardust of dying stars. In that sense, we are truly connected, woven from the same cosmic tapestry.

Though our expressions of faith may vary in customs and rituals, the core truth might be the same: a universe filled with wonder and a place where we can all find peace and safety, regardless of how we choose to acknowledge the creative spark that binds us all.

We have all been created from stardust—made from the death of millions of stars. Stars died but lived again, like you and me. We are "one," all of us. We may look, dress, and talk differently, but we are all the same.

Perhaps a shift could occur if we embraced a deeper understanding of our shared origin. Imagine a world where judgment dissolves, replaced by acceptance—acceptance of one another and even of those who walk among you from beyond your planet. This acceptance wouldn't erase the rich tapestry of cultures and beliefs that make your world unique. Instead, it could serve as a bridge, allowing you to celebrate your commonalities while appreciating the beauty of your differences.

The concept of "special" often leads to division. Perhaps a more empowering perspective exists: that we are all unique expressions of the same creative force, each playing a vital role in the grand play of existence. On your world, this journey of growth can be especially challenging. We hold immense respect for those who

21

choose to experience this "Earth school," with all its complexities. We have witnessed your struggles, but we also see your remarkable potential. While we won't directly intervene, we offer a watchful presence, knowing that the time for many to return "home" draws closer.

Communication – 08/21/2022 between Gorto and Writer

Writer: So I find the time and space to come again and continue our conversation. What would you like me to know?

Gorto: There is so much to share and so much to download so you can communicate with others. Where do we begin? There are many channelers out there that speak with us on a daily basis. So much is shared, but I would like to speak of building the bridge tonight. What would our bridge look like? No, not stairs to heaven; that would be a very long climb from your earth to ours. There is no way to build a span over a body of water to connect our two land masses; how do you visualize a bridge? Is there any bridge on your earth?

W: I would see a sturdy bridge made of large planks of weathered wood. Much like any dock you would see by the ocean. Large round pylons from which to string a hearty rope in case one might start to fall. Much like the bridge to heaven that my daughter drew for the Children's book.

Or, I would see a bridge as nothing more than a pathway leading from here to there. I could see us walking from each direction towards each other, meeting in the middle, where we greet each other with an embrace. I see a mass of people surrounding us, lining both sides of the pathway. I hear murmurs from the crowd of fear, not knowing what will happen but waiting to see, curious as well as fearful.
And do we meet?

G: Of course, we do, for I am you, and you are me, and together we are one in spirit. I come in peace; you come in peace. We each bring a lit torch to guide us to each other, not that it is dark and we can't see the way, but to ensure that our way is lighted for all to see from a great distance. I see us come together to greet one another, hands on our hearts, for we are brothers and sisters of the creator God who made us.

W: We exchange torches, signifying that each way has been accepted. Holding hands, we turn in each direction, holding our torches high for all to see. Slowly, others from the crowds, those who are not afraid, begin to walk towards us, bowing to honor our leadership and uniting your people and our people.

Turning around, those coming forward stand with us, showing the others that there is nothing to

23

fear, that a bridge between the Star Beings and humans has been built, crossed, and is now strong and accepting of all. The sharing has begun between all races who are willing to learn from the teachers of the future. I see peace.

G: *And so it is that it happens just that way. A perfect bridge, a perfect ending. Together, we go forth and teach those willing to learn and hear our stories as well as those we write together. That is the beautiful new world coming.*

W: So how do we get there? Where do we go from here?

G: *Let it begin . . . Once upon a time, in a star galaxy far, far away . . .*

Why Build A Bridge Of Communication

The question of why aliens would want to build a bridge of communication between us is a very intriguing and complex one, and there is no definitive or conclusive answer to it. However, based on some web search results, I can offer you some possible reasons or motives that aliens may have for contacting or communicating with us.

I am not a fan of bold fonts and bullets, and I recognize that sometimes they can detract from the reading ease, but there is so much information to share concerning communication concerns that I ask for your indulgence concerning this topic.

Some possible reasons are:

- Curiosity and exploration. Aliens may want to communicate with us because they are curious and interested in learning more about us, our planet, our culture, our history, and our science. They may also want to share their own knowledge and experience with us and exchange ideas and perspectives.
- Cooperation and collaboration. Aliens may want to communicate with us because they seek cooperation and collaboration for mutual benefit or common goals. They may want to establish diplomatic or trade relations or join forces to solve global or cosmic problems, such as environmental issues, resource scarcity, or existential threats.
- Education and enlightenment. Aliens may want to communicate with us because they are trying to educate and enlighten us, for our own good or for theirs. They may want to help us improve our

technology, society, or spirituality or correct our mistakes or misconceptions. They may also want to test or challenge our intelligence, morality, or creativity.

- Manipulation and domination. Aliens may want to communicate with us because they are aiming to manipulate and dominate us for their own benefit or agenda. They may want to deceive, exploit, or enslave us or to take over our planet, resources, or DNA. They may also want to impose their culture, religion, or ideology on us or to eliminate or assimilate us.

What they might share: They could potentially offer insights into physics, mathematics, or understanding the universe that could revolutionize our scientific understanding. Sharing their experiences and knowledge of the cosmos could broaden our view of the universe's vastness and the potential existence of other intelligent life. Perhaps they could emphasize the importance of concepts like peace, cooperation, or sustainability that transcend cultural boundaries.

What we might share to encourage contact: Showcasing advancements in areas like renewable energy, space exploration, or peaceful conflict resolution could indicate our potential for positive contributions. Efforts like developing universal communication methods or transmitting messages through radio telescopes could signal our willingness to establish contact. Overcoming significant international conflicts and demonstrating a commitment to collective problem-solving could portray us as a more unified and mature civilization.

Why they might want to contact us: A desire to advance the collective knowledge of the universe and foster understanding between different species. Offering guidance or assistance to a younger civilization facing challenges. Potential concerns about existential threats or ensuring the peaceful development of civilizations within the galaxy.

Unforeseen Consequences Of Worldwide Contact

When I began thinking about presenting my star being friends to the world and sharing with my readers how to make contact with them, I had to stop and think about not only the positive effect it could have on our culture and civilization but also what damage could be done if things went wrong with the introduction. That is why this book sat in draft on my shelf for the past year—I didn't want to expose my friends to the hatred and fear experienced today.

Then Gorto met with me, expressing the need to hurry this information along as contact will be soon. "When is 'soon'? you ask – "*soon.*" So I dug deep and decided to look at and present my thoughts on what could go wrong and what I was praying for to go right. I know my star being friends will protect us all, or they wouldn't have asked for this meeting.

Misunderstandings and Cultural Clashes: Even with advanced technology, deciphering their communication methods and overcoming cultural differences could lead to misinterpretations and misunderstandings. Our priorities and motivations might vastly differ from theirs, potentially leading to conflict or a sense of exploitation. Access to vastly superior technology could lead to dependence, hindering our own technological development and fostering a culture of relying on external solutions. Advanced technology in the wrong hands, even unintentionally, could pose an existential threat if not handled cautiously.

Societal Disruption and Loss of Identity: Over-reliance on their knowledge and solutions could hinder our ability to solve problems independently and weaken our societal resilience. Exposure to a vastly different civilization might lead to a loss of our own cultural values and traditions.

Unforeseen Biological or Environmental Consequences: The unintentional transfer of microorganisms or biological materials could have devastating consequences for both civilizations. Their presence or actions, even with good intentions, could have unforeseen ecological repercussions on our planet.

Existential Threats: While unlikely, the possibility of encountering a civilization with hostile intentions cannot be entirely ruled out. Even with peaceful intentions, their advanced technology could pose an unforeseen existential threat due to a simple misunderstanding.

The revelation of extraterrestrial intelligence could cause widespread societal unease, panic, or religious upheaval. A significant technological gap could create a power imbalance, potentially leading to a manipulative or exploitative dynamic.

Striving for peaceful coexistence, international cooperation, and sustainable practices strengthens our civilization as a whole. Prioritizing scientific research could equip us to understand the universe better and potentially prepare for any future encounters, should they occur. Open contact with star beings, while a thought-provoking concept, holds potential benefits and significant risks. Focusing on our advancement as a responsible and peaceful species remains paramount.

Unforeseen Consequences of Individual Contact

While individual contact with a star being might seem like a less risky scenario compared to global contact, it still presents significant uncertainties and potential consequences.

Our current knowledge about star beings is purely hypothetical. Their motivations, communication methods, and the potential outcomes of individual interaction remain entirely speculative. An individual encounter with a vastly superior being could result in overwhelming psychological trauma or mental instability, even if the star being has benevolent intentions.

An individual's account of contact might be interpreted as delusion, hallucination, or fabricated story due to the lack of objective evidence.
False claims or misinterpretations of the encounter could spread panic or confusion within the wider population.

Individual actions, misunderstandings, or even cultural differences could inadvertently provoke a negative response from the star being. The individual might be subjected to unknown influences or manipulation by the superior being, even if initially perceived as positive.

While individual contact might seem less catastrophic than global contact, it still carries significant risks due to the unknown nature of star beings and the potential psychological and societal consequences.

As discussed earlier, focusing on our civilization's development through scientific advancement, peaceful conflict resolution, and environmental responsibility might better prepare us for potential future encounters, should they occur. Research aimed at understanding the universe, exoplanets, and the possibility of extraterrestrial life can be pursued through a collective global effort.

While individual contact with a star being might seem like a less risky scenario compared to global contact, it still presents significant uncertainties and potential consequences:

Our current knowledge about star beings is purely hypothetical for most. However, for those of us who believe because we "know" of their existence, their motivations, communication methods, and the potential outcomes of individual interaction remain entirely speculative in the long run. An individual encounter with a vastly superior being could result in overwhelming psychological trauma or mental instability, even if the star being has benevolent intentions.

The Power of Belief

I would be remiss if I did not approach this story from both a scientific and a metaphysical perspective. As an archaeologist at heart, I believe in a multifaceted approach, providing a look at this phenomenon with an open mind and a willingness to explore the unknown.

Even without incontrovertible scientific proof, belief in star beings can be a powerful force for some people. It can inspire curiosity about the universe, a sense of connection to something greater than ourselves, and a hope for discovering intelligent life.

Finding Balance

The ideal approach might be a balance between open-mindedness and healthy skepticism. Being receptive to possibilities without abandoning critical thinking can lead to a more nuanced understanding of the universe and our place within it. Scientific events that could establish evidence of star beings:

The most impactful evidence would be a clear, unambiguous signal from space containing information demonstrating intelligence. This could include complex mathematical structures, coded messages, or a universal language beyond human understanding.

Finding unexplained structures on planets or moons, like massive buildings or advanced technology beyond human capabilities, could point toward extraterrestrial intelligence.

Direct physical contact with star beings, whether through travel to their planet or their arrival on Earth, would be undeniable evidence. This would require communication and interaction to confirm sentience and intelligence.

If we observed spaceships with capabilities far exceeding ours traveling through space, it could strongly suggest the existence of a more advanced civilization.

Universal Laws and Physics: Discovering previously unknown laws of physics or universal constants that explain the existence of intelligent life elsewhere could be evidence.

Finding evidence of life on other planets, especially if it displays biosignatures significantly different from life on Earth, could suggest another origin or contact with extraterrestrial organisms.

Any evidence should be verifiable and repeatable by multiple independent research groups to avoid misinterpretation or hoaxes.

The meaning of evidence depends on interpretation. For example, a simple signal might be a natural phenomenon, while a complex message would be more substantial evidence.

Scientists are actively searching for evidence of extraterrestrial intelligence through projects like SETI and studying exoplanets. While we haven't found conclusive evidence yet, the possibilities remain exciting!

How Humans Without A Strictly Scientific Mindset Might Be Convinced Of Star Beings

For those less inclined towards a purely scientific worldview, the possibility of star beings can be a compelling belief. Encounters, of any kind can spark this conviction. Setting an intention to connect with a star being, for instance, might lead to an experience that resonates with that desire. Similarly, recurring dreams or visions, especially shared by multiple people, can foster a strong sense of their reality.

Unexplained phenomena like UFO sightings, feelings of being watched, or even telepathic communication can all be interpreted as contact with these advanced beings. Existing religious or spiritual traditions that already embrace extraterrestrial beings or higher dimensions provide fertile ground for such experiences to be seen as confirmation. Ultimately, some people trust their intuition and inner feelings, feeling a deep conviction in the presence of star beings even without concrete proof.

Personal experiences can be subjective and influenced by expectations or psychology. Verification through multiple witnesses or physical evidence is important. We tend to interpret information in a way that confirms our existing beliefs. Being critical and open to alternative explanations is essential. Hoaxes or misinterpretations can cloud the issue. Investigating sources and remaining skeptical are important.

Significant Risks For Both Star Beings And Humans

Even entertaining the hypothetical scenario of confirmed extraterrestrial life (ET), encouraging contact carries significant risks for both them and humans:

Even if peaceful, our intentions might be misconstrued as hostile or self-serving due to vast cultural and technological differences. Our presence could inadvertently disrupt their societal balance or introduce contaminants harmful to their environment or biology.

Dangers for Humans: Their vastly advanced technology could be misused intentionally or unintentionally, posing an existential threat. Their advanced society might inadvertently impose their belief systems or practices, leading to the loss of their cultural identity. The revelation of a superior species could cause widespread anxiety, panic, or societal upheaval.

Humans, with our current state of societal progress, might be vulnerable to manipulation or control by a more advanced civilization. Even with good intentions, cross-species interaction could trigger unforeseen consequences with far-reaching implications for both parties.

While the desire for contact is understandable, encouraging it without proper preparation and understanding of the potential consequences is imprudent.

Investing in research aimed at understanding the universe, exoplanets, and potential communication methods would be a more responsible step. Prioritizing peaceful international relations, sustainable development, and ethical advancement strengthens our civilization as a whole.

Importance of Scientific Inquiry: Contacting an unknown advanced species should not be driven by individual motivations. A collective global effort through scientific research organizations should lay the groundwork for potential future communication, ensuring it's conducted with caution and proper understanding.

While the possibility of extraterrestrial life is intriguing, scientific evidence currently doesn't support their existence. Focusing our efforts on responsible scientific inquiry and societal advancement positions us better for any future encounters, should they occur.

I think science already knows they are here. Is it possible the government doesn't want to let on they are here so other nations won't try to steal our alien technology?

There's no definitive scientific evidence conclusively proving the existence of extraterrestrial beings interacting with Earth. While speculation about government knowledge exists, no credible evidence supports a global cover-up regarding extraterrestrial life. Or does it?

Given the unknown nature of potential extraterrestrial beings and the hypothesized risks discussed earlier, humanity currently lacks the scientific understanding and global coordination necessary for safe and responsible contact. Attributing government silence solely to protecting alien technology from other nations rests on unsubstantiated claims. Scientific research aimed at understanding the universe and the possibility of extraterrestrial life should guide our approach.

Open communication within the scientific community and international cooperation is crucial for responsible exploration of this field.

Addressing the possibility: While the concept of extraterrestrial life is intriguing, prioritizing evidence-based scientific inquiry over speculation is essential. It's important to acknowledge:

Scientific organizations like SETI (Search for Extraterrestrial Intelligence) are dedicated to the scientific search for extraterrestrial life. Disclosure of incontrovertible evidence of extraterrestrial life would likely spark global discussions and international collaboration on how to proceed with such an unprecedented discovery.

Addressing Human Fears of Actual Contact

Hollywood's Impact On The American Psyche On E.T.S

I discussed the importance of what I consider the most famous movie from my perspective, *"The Day the Earth Stood Still (1950),* in the Preface and the effect it had on the awakening of my involvement with the star beings.

But there were more, and Hollywood went out of its way to fulfill its agenda of creating fear. Perhaps many of you saw some of these movies more as thrillers; others saw the possibilities of a future involving space.

While a definitive count is difficult, films portraying aliens as fearful beings are significantly more common than positive portrayals. Here's a breakdown of some of the more well-known movies:

Dominant Trend: Fearful Aliens: Movies like "*War of the Worlds*" (1953), "*Independence Day*" (1996), and "*Mars Attacks!*" (1996) depict aliens as hostile invaders seeking to conquer or destroy Earth. Films like "*Alien*" (1979), "*The Thing*" (1982), and countless B-movies establish aliens as monstrous threats with little to no positive attributes.

Why create fear? Our lack of knowledge about extraterrestrial life fuels anxieties, making them easy targets for portrayal as dangerous. Invasion and horror stories involving aliens provide a sense of excitement and adrenaline rush for audiences. The "alien menace" trope is ingrained in popular culture, offering a familiar framework for storytelling.

41

Examples of Positive Portrayals (Exist, but Less Common): *E.T. the Extraterrestrial (1982)*: This heartwarming film portrays an alien being as a gentle and vulnerable creature seeking to return home. *Arrival (2016)*: This thought-provoking film focuses on communication and understanding between humans and aliens with a complex message. *Star Trek Franchise*: This long-running series features various alien species, some with whom humans have peaceful interactions and even alliances.

Starman (1984) is a classic alien encounter film with a heartwarming message about humanity. Here's how it portrays humanity:

As a flawed but hopeful species, the film doesn't shy away from showing human flaws like fear, suspicion, and the desire for control when faced with the unknown. The government's pursuit of Starman reflects these tendencies.

Despite initial apprehension, the protagonist, Jenny Hayden (played by Karen Allen), develops a genuine connection with Starman. Their journey together showcases human kindness, compassion, and the ability to overcome fear through understanding.

Starman's quest to understand humanity highlights our inherent curiosity and desire for connection with something beyond ourselves.

The film portrays Starman learning about human emotions, particularly love and loss, which creates an emotional bond between him and Jenny. This shows that some core human experiences are universal, even across species.

"Starman" ultimately delivers a message of hope and possibility. It suggests that despite our flaws, humanity can empathize, connect, and wonder. The film celebrates the potential for understanding and even love to bridge the gap between humans and extraterrestrials.

Shifting Landscape: Movies like *"Avatar" (2009)* explore the potential for conflict arising from cultural clashes rather than inherent alien hostility. Some films depict attempts to understand alien motivations and establish peaceful coexistence.

Science Fiction Exploration: On the surface, *"Enemy Mine"* (1985) explores themes common in science fiction: space exploration, first contact with alien life, and the struggle for survival on a hostile planet. The film delves deeper into character development and the power of overcoming prejudice. The initial animosity between the human and alien characters leads to cooperation and even friendship.

The central message revolves around breaking down barriers and finding common ground despite differences. The stranded human and alien are forced to rely on each other for survival, leading them to appreciate their different strengths and perspectives.

The film emphasizes the value of empathy and understanding. The characters overcome their initial fear and suspicion by learning about each other's cultures and motivations. In the end, "*Enemy Mine*" showcases the power of connection that can blossom even in the most unexpected circumstances. The human and alien forge a strong bond despite their contrasting appearances and backgrounds.

Finding the Balance: While the unknown aspects of alien life can be a source of fear, scientific exploration encourages a more nuanced approach. Films can portray a wider range of alien species with diverse characteristics and motivations. "*Close Encounters of the Third Kind*" (1977) deserves a spot on this list! It's a landmark science fiction film by Steven Spielberg that explores humanity's first attempt to communicate with extraterrestrial intelligence.

"*Close Encounters*" is widely considered a critical and commercial success. It's praised for its visuals, sense of wonder, and groundbreaking special effects. "*Close Encounters*" doesn't portray a clear-cut message of fear or encouragement. Instead, it explores the awe-inspiring mystery of potential contact. The film depicts initial anxieties and confusion surrounding the UFO sightings, but the overall tone shifts towards wonder and curiosity as humanity attempts communication. The iconic ending sequence at Devil's Tower is a hopeful depiction of interspecies understanding.

"*Close Encounters*" is a film that captures the complex emotions surrounding the possibility of encountering alien intelligence – a mix of apprehension, curiosity, and, ultimately, the hope for connection.

A small but growing number challenge this stereotype; as our understanding of the universe evolves, films can potentially depict aliens in a more balanced and diverse light.

It's important to acknowledge that films often reflect cultural anxieties and societal perceptions. The prevalence of fearful portrayals of aliens might indicate a collective unease with the unknown. As scientific research progresses and our understanding of the universe expands, the portrayal of aliens in films could gradually shift toward a more nuanced and diverse representation.

One last thought: What in humans or human nature allows one to find the concept of alien life impossible? Fear of retaliation from whom? Fear of realizing what they have been conditioned to believe might be wrong. Religious beliefs? Science? Most people could care less about scientific facts. There has to be something else—what is that something else?

Some factors that contribute to the difficulty some people have accepting the concept of alien life:

1. Absence of conclusive evidence: Humans are naturally drawn to concrete evidence. The lack of incontrovertible proof of extraterrestrial life makes the concept difficult to grasp for some.

2. Unfamiliarity and the unknown: Our current understanding of life is based on observations of Earth.

The idea of life forms existing beyond our known biological parameters can be challenging to fathom.

3. Psychological discomfort: The vastness of the universe and the possibility of advanced alien civilizations can be overwhelming and even frightening for some individuals.

4. Cultural and religious beliefs: Long-held belief systems and cultural narratives may not readily accommodate the concept of extraterrestrial intelligence.

5. Misinformation and sensationalized portrayals: Negative media representations of aliens often focus on hostile invasion scenarios, fueling fears and skepticism.

Addressing specific points: Fear of retaliation: While the unknown can be unsettling, the scientific community generally approaches the search for extraterrestrial life with curiosity and a desire for peaceful communication.

Fear of the unknown: Scientific inquiry aims to gradually unravel the mysteries of the universe, including the potential existence of alien life.

Religious beliefs: Many religious beliefs are adapting to the possibility of extraterrestrial life, focusing on the universality of existence and creation. While science plays a crucial role, Cultural narratives, personal beliefs, and media portrayals also influence public perception. Open and honest discussions about the limitations of our current knowledge and the ongoing search for evidence are essential.

It's important to note many people are intrigued by the possibility of alien life and actively support scientific efforts aimed at discovery.

Curiosity and a willingness to consider new information are key to advancing our understanding of the universe. Scientific progress often challenges existing beliefs. History is filled with examples of assumptions overturned by new discoveries. As we continue exploring the universe, the possibility of finding evidence of alien life should not be dismissed solely due to fear or unfamiliarity. A balance between healthy skepticism and open-mindedness is needed as scientific inquiry unfolds.

CHAPTER 3

History and Evolution of Extraterrestrials

"Star Being" V.S. "Starborn"

Is there a difference between the terms "star being" and "starborn?" The terms *star being* and *starborn* are both used to refer to beings who have transcended their original form and become connected to the multiverse. However, they seem to have different connotations and origins.

Star being is a more general term that can apply to any being connected to the stars, whether they are human, alien, or something else. Star beings may have different origins, such as ancient civilizations, cosmic experiments, or spiritual awakenings. Star beings may also have different purposes, such as spreading messages, guiding humanity, or exploring the universe.

Starborn, on the other hand, is a more specific term. Starborn are beings who have stepped into Unity, a device that allows them to access the infinite possibilities of the multiverse. Starborns are essentially reborn in a new universe where they can repeat or change their choices. Starborn is also opposed by the Constellation, a faction that seeks to preserve the original timeline.

Therefore, the difference between star being and starborn is that star being is a broader and more inclusive term, while starborn is a narrower and more exclusive term. The usage of these terms may depend on the context and the preference of the speaker. Some may identify as both, while others may prefer one over the other.

I use either term interchangeably throughout the book.

Star beings, also known as aliens, extraterrestrials, or ETs, are life forms that originate from other planets, stars, or galaxies. The history and evolution of star beings are unknown, but what is shared by many entities to channelers and messengers on Earth, as there is no conclusive evidence or scientific consensus that they exist or have ever contacted us? *"However, many theories, speculations, and stories attempt to explain or imagine the origin, nature, and diversity of star beings based on various sources of inspiration, such*

as astronomy, biology, physics, psychology, religion, mythology, and culture.[9]

Theories abound on the history and evolution of these enigmatic star beings. Some propose they arose from the same primordial soup that birthed life on Earth, only under vastly different conditions in far-flung corners of the cosmos. This idea suggests a dazzling diversity of forms and adaptations driven by the unique environments they call home.

Others believe star beings are the descendants or creations of ancient civilizations, perhaps predating humanity or existing alongside us for a time. For reasons of war, disaster, exploration, or perhaps even transcendence, these civilizations may have left Earth or chosen to remain hidden. This theory resonates with those who believe in a rich, hidden history filled with secrets waiting to be uncovered, secrets that could reveal our true origins and place in the vast universe.

Finally, some posit star beings as products of higher dimensions, parallel universes, or alternative

---

[9] Star - Formation, Evolution, Lifecycle | Britannica

realities. These beings might interact with our physical world through wormholes, portals, or even psychic phenomena, their influence veiled from our limited perception.

Many of us feel a connection to the stars, a sense that we are not alone in this vast universe. We wonder if there are other beings out there who share our ancestry or destiny. Some call them star beings, the offspring or creations of ancient civilizations that coexisted with or preceded humanity on Earth. These star beings may have left our planet or hidden themselves for various reasons, such as conflict, catastrophe, exploration, or ascension. We believe that there is a deeper history, full of secrets and mysteries, that could reveal our true origins and purpose. We eagerly await the day when we can uncover these hidden truths and discover the wonders that have always been beyond our reach.

These are just some of the possible scenarios people have imagined or speculated about the history and evolution of star beings, etc. However, none of these scenarios are based on empirical evidence or scientific consensus, and they may reflect more on our hopes, fears, and fantasies than on the reality of the situation.

Biologically Speaking

The answer is not very clear because there is no scientific evidence that extraterrestrials exist or have visited Earth. However, there is a lot of speculation and imagination about what they might look like and how they might be classified. Some entities are reported to have very different physical, mental, and cultural characteristics from humans.

One way to approach the question is to use the concept of biological species, which is a group of organisms that can interbreed and produce fertile offspring. However, this concept may not apply to extraterrestrials, who may have very different origins, genetics, and modes of reproduction from Earth life. "Moreover, some extraterrestrials, such as robots or cyborgs, may be artificial and not belong to any biological species."[10]

---

[10] https://en.wikipedia.org/wiki/extraterrestial_life

Cultural Races

Another way to approach the question is to use the concept of cultural race, a social construct categorizing people based on physical or cultural traits. However, this concept is also problematic, as it is not based on clear or objective criteria and may reflect human biases and prejudices. It would not be uncommon to find extraterrestrials appearing as energy beings or collective minds, not fitting into any racial categories.

Therefore, the question of whether there are different races or species of extraterrestrials is not easy to answer and may depend on how one defines and identifies extraterrestrials. There may be many diverse and complex forms of extraterrestrial life in the universe, but it is also possible that there are none at all.

If you want to learn more about star beings, etc., check out these websites: [SETI Institute], [Ancient Aliens], and [Multiverse Theory].

"Races"/"Species" – How Each Came About

The concept of "one race" equals "humanity" can be based on scientific and biological evidence, as all humans belong to the same species and share the same genetic makeup. There is no basis for dividing humans into different races since individual variation is more evident in the groups. Race is, and will always be, a social construct rather than a scientific one.

The concept of "star beings" or "starseeds" is based on the spiritual and metaphysical belief that some souls originate from other planets, stars, or dimensions and incarnate on Earth to help with their evolution. These souls are said to have different characteristics and abilities depending on their origin and are often referred to as different "races" or "types" of starseeds.[11] However, this does not mean that they are biologically different from human beings, as they still have human bodies and DNA. They are spiritually different, with different memories, missions, and connections to other realms.

Therefore, "one race" and "star beings" are not contradictory but complementary. They reflect different aspects of our existence: the physical and the

---

[11] https://www.livescience.com/47627-race-is-not-a-science-concept.html

metaphysical, the scientific and the spiritual, the earthly and the cosmic. We are all one human race but also diverse and unique starseeds. We are all connected, but we also have our own journeys. We are all part of the same source but also have our own expressions.

Many diverse resources have described Star beings as *otherworldly beings from different star systems and planets all over the universe.* I will discuss those I am most connected to—those coming from the more well-known places such as Pleiades, Sirius, Lyrans, Andromeda, and Arcturus.

To explain the different names of the different groups of star beings, one must know that 1) there is diversity and complexity among the star beings and that they have different names to reflect their unique qualities and missions. 2) There is a connection and a similarity among the star beings. They have different names to express their varied perspectives and experiences. 3) There is a possibility and a mystery among star beings; they have different names to reveal their hidden secrets and potentials.

Throughout my research of the various star being names, I found numerous resources (websites, etc.), each claiming a definition or explanation "as their own" when, in fact, I can see the same information (often the exact verbiage without citations) on each of the different websites. Therefore, I have listed all the website resources I encountered under my book's Resources section to alleviate the need for many footnotes. I mean, no disrespect to each author claiming their definition is original; I have no way of figuring out whose definition is the true original.

Different names for the different groups of star beings. The most common differences are not indicative of their race but rather their culture, history, and mission. Star beings have different ways of expressing their identity and purpose. Often, a shared common ancestry or origin could have diverged over time. Migration, intervention, and evolution are a few reasons for this divergence. Some groups are said to be related. But have distinctive characteristics and roles. Andromedans are also known as Celestials (Angels) because of their high vibrational frequency and divine connections throughout history. Arcturians are known as the Elders or the Ancient Ones because of their advanced age and wisdom.

Star Beings and the Echoes of the Past

Many cultures have woven stories and legends of star beings or extraterrestrial visitors into the fabric of their traditions. These narratives hold deep meaning and offer a glimpse into how these societies viewed the cosmos and humanity's place within it. For instance, Cherokee legends speak of Native American origins in the Pleiades star cluster, portraying them as "star seeds" entrusted with spreading knowledge and light.[12] Similarly, Buddhist teachings encompass the existence of Buddhas residing in various worlds. Additionally, petroglyphs left behind by Indigenous peoples depict encounters with enigmatic aircraft and non-human beings of unknown origin. These beings, often referred

---

[12] https://atmos.earth/ancient-ties-indigenous-people-and-the-extraterrestrial/

to as "Sky People" or "Star People," hold a prominent place in the lore of many Native American nations.[13]

Across the globe, ancient civilizations like the Egyptians, Sumerians, and Mayans shared a belief in their gods or ancestors hailing from the stars or other planets. Artifacts unearthed by archaeologists, including petroglyphs and various other objects, are interpreted by some as hinting at the presence of extraterrestrial beings. However, for many, the existence of extraterrestrial life remains contingent on concrete scientific evidence, such as direct observation, communication, or confirmed contact.

Lack of personal relevance. Some people may not be interested or invested in the topic of extraterrestrial life as they do not see how it affects or relates to their own lives, values, or beliefs. They may have other priorities or concerns that occupy their attention and energy, such as their family, work, health, or hobbies. They may also have a different worldview or faith that does not accommodate or

---

[13] https://atmos.earth/ancient-ties-indigenous-people-and-the-extraterrestrial/digenous Peoples and the Extraterrestrial | Atmos

support the idea of extraterrestrial life or considers it irrelevant or insignificant. Therefore, some people may not believe in the existence of extraterrestrial life because they do not care or feel connected to it.

Fear of the unknown. Some people may be afraid or uncomfortable with the idea of extraterrestrial life, as they perceive it as a threat or a challenge to their security, identity, or status. They may worry that extraterrestrial life could harm or invade us or that it could expose or undermine our ignorance or inferiority. They may also resist or reject any change or innovation that could disrupt or transform their familiar and established way of life. Therefore, some people may not believe in the existence of extraterrestrial life because they want to avoid or deny it.

These are just some of the possible reasons why some people may not believe in the existence of extraterrestrial life despite the archaeological finds and stories that you mentioned. However, these reasons are not necessarily valid or rational, and they may reflect more on their personal biases, emotions, or preferences than on the reality of the situation. Therefore, they should not discourage or dissuade you from pursuing your curiosity and fascination with the topic as long as you do so with an open mind and a critical eye.

Some modern cultures, such as the Raelians, the Scientologists, and Heaven's Gate, believe that star beings or extraterrestrials are humanity's creators, guides, or saviors and that they will return or reveal themselves in the future.[14]

These are just some examples of different cultures' stories or beliefs about star beings or extraterrestrials.

---

[14] https://atmos.earth/ancient-ties-indigenous-people-and-the-extraterrestrial/digenous Peoples and the Extraterrestrial | Atmos

CHAPTER 4

Understanding Star-Being Communication

*The difference between us is that I
remember my gift,
You have forgotten yours.
Find your gift now as we travel through
time and space
to the other side of the veil.*
-"Writer"

Communicating With the World of Spirit

I have been communicating with the spirit world since I was born. I never questioned my ability to speak with or see spirits, those children, adults, or animals whose life energy had left their bodies and moved to the nonphysical plane or "the other side." I didn't understand why adults didn't see or hear them. Then, when I was ten, my father was killed, and I shut down my communication with the world of spirit.

1994, as an adult, I began to allow spirit communication back into my life when I connected with two earthbound spirit children at my home in Idaho. But it wasn't until one day in 2007, as I sat on a beach in Cape Cod, counting the waves and seeking change and healing, that I realized communicating with the world of spirit and sharing those messages with others must be a way back to living the life I was meant to live. I listened.

Each of us, not just me, came into this lifetime knowing that we could communicate with the spirit world. When we were young, the veil between the spirit home we had just left and our new, earthly home was thin. Not only do we communicate with those spirits we've left behind, but our soul also moves freely between the two dimensions. We are encouraged and supported if we are born into a family accepting our ability to communicate telepathically with spirits. If not, we bow to social and parental pressures, wrapping our knowledge in an oilskin and tucking it away in our secret box where it will be safe until we can use it again.

How I communicate with spirits resembles what we think of as telepathy, or the exchange of information through thought. Telepathic communication has been going on in various cultures since the beginning of time as we know it. Considered a universal ability, telepathy is shared by all as inhabitants of Mother Earth. Before there was a vocal spoken language, telepathic communication—or "mind talk," as I call it—was all there was.

I communicate with the world of spirit using the three most common forms of spiritual communication:

Clairvoyance (visual communication) allows us to see others' thoughts or information not necessarily with our physical eyes but rather as colors, forms, and textures in our mind's eye (also known as the third eye). For example, I see entities or spirits as if they were fully embodied people standing right in front of me.

Clairaudience (auditory communication) allows us to hear others' thoughts or receive information not with our physical ears but as voices in our minds. When I speak with spirits, I listen to what they are saying as clearly as I hear people speaking in ordinary reality. The voices of the spirits I hear sound just like those of people I speak with in regular conversations, but I listen to their voices with the same clarity.

Clairsentience (tactile communication), in which we pick up thoughts and information and convert them into a feeling, be it emotional or physical. You may feel the information as calming feelings, as a prickly sensation, or as the hairs on your arms and back of your neck standing up. As you begin to differentiate types of spiritual energies, you will come to recognize the different feelings or sensations each trigger for you. For example, my legs tingle when I am in a spiritual entity's presence. I can also tell whether an entity has left a physical body and is now on the other side or is still inhabiting a body on the physical plane and using the world of spirit to communicate with me by how heavy or dense its energy feels.

The spirits that "come through" the spiritual world to me may be those who have left their physical bodies and now are back home in the world of spirit, or they may still be inhabiting physical bodies here on Earth but have left their bodies temporarily to meet me on the nonphysical, spiritual plane.

When I telepathically talk with the spirits that come to me, I can only describe my consciousness as a deep meditative state. While my physical body remains in the chair on the physical plane, my soul is in the nonphysical realm, acting as an observer and participant on the nonphysical plane. There, I am able to interact with spirits as if we both were still in physical bodies. I see/visualize each spirit as an image with a face and a body. I see their essence, their aura (energy field). Linear time passes while I am away from the physical, though I am unaware of its passing. Depending upon how much time I have spent away from my physical body, it can take some time for me to readjust to it when I return.

Communication with the world of spirit can be done at any time, any place. It doesn't require anything other than for you to show up and ask questions with respect and appreciation. Communicating with spiritual beings—whether they are angels and fairies, the spirits of children or soldiers who have died, or the spirits of animals, rocks, or trees—is as simple as sitting quietly and allowing yourself to hear or see what they would have you know. Their voices are, quite simply, the still, small voice you hear in your head, see in your mind's eye, or feel with your body or emotions.

My work with the world of spirit is inspired by a higher power, which I know as "God." Not the "God" of religion, but rather the Creator God with whom and from whom it all began. Bringing forth spirit stories in a published format is my way of saying, "I am a communicator with the world of spirit. This is who I am and what I do." As our soul moves into greater spiritual evolution, I believe it is important to see more communication accounts with the world of spirit in written form so that others might realize this communication is possible.

Spirituality and Star Beings. I believe that God speaks to and through each of us in many ways—including through the voices of those in the spirit world—in an attempt to remind us of the home we left behind when our souls chose to incarnate into physical bodies.

The time is coming when "We will need their friendship and assistance to save ourselves in the end." This in no way is asking you to leave your belief in God, a supreme being called by many different names by different cultures and civilizations. "God" is the name of one of many ascended masters. Jesus himself is a star being, and it was the day he became "real" for me. Why, you might ask – I am willing and more likely to follow a teacher who has, with an open mind, studied all the teachings available to bring a universal view of life for his message.

Many religions and spiritual teachings emphasize the importance of love and light. Benevolent star beings, if they exist, might share this core message of promoting love, understanding, and unity among all beings. Figures like Jesus and Buddha stressed the importance of compassion and service to others. This aligns with the potential mission of helpful star beings who might wish to uplift humanity. The concept of spiritual growth is present in many traditions.

Ascended masters, perhaps advanced beings from other worlds, might play a role in guiding humanity's spiritual evolution, preparing us for potential contact with star beings. Instead of viewing ascended masters solely through a religious lens, we can consider them as highly evolved beings who have transcended physical limitations. This concept aligns with the idea of advanced star beings who possess greater knowledge and wisdom.

Perhaps some of the figures we revere as ascended masters were actually star beings who visited Earth in the past. They might have come to share knowledge, guide our spiritual development, and lay the groundwork for future contact with their kind.

Jesus as Star Being and Advanced Soul. Some believe Jesus was not simply a human teacher but an advanced soul who came to Earth with a specific mission. His teachings on love, forgiveness, and helping others resonate with the potential goals of benevolent star beings who might wish to see humanity evolve toward greater compassion and unity. The teachings of Jesus on love, forgiveness, and helping others align with the potential message of benevolent star beings. Perhaps these are universal values that resonate across different worlds and civilizations.

Many spiritual traditions speak of advanced souls who choose to incarnate on Earth to guide humanity's evolution. The teachings of Jesus, emphasizing love, forgiveness, and spiritual growth, resonate with these concepts. While some might call Jesus' acts miracles, perhaps they can be seen as demonstrations of advanced abilities developed through a deep understanding of the universe's energy and potential.

Jesus' mission on Earth, filled with compassion and sacrifice, aligns with the potential role of an advanced soul who wishes to uplift humanity toward a higher state of being.

There are many different beliefs about God, Jesus, and ascended masters. I respect these figures' diverse interpretations of various religions and spiritual paths. While specific beliefs may differ, there are underlying themes of love, compassion, and spiritual growth that many traditions share. These universals might also be reflected in the intentions of benevolent star beings who wish to see humanity progress.

Many ancient cultures have stories of visitation from heavenly beings. Perhaps these accounts, reinterpreted through a modern lens, could be seen as encounters with advanced star beings from other worlds. In my own experiences, I have felt a connection between the presence of star beings and the teachings of love and compassion. However, I understand that these experiences are unique to me and may not be shared by everyone.

Having said all that, these pages will tell a slightly different story as they deal with communication between living entities of different dimensions. These entities are known by different names. Some call them Aliens or Extraterrestrials—I call them Star Beings and Starborns, but mostly, I call them my family.

CHAPTER 5

Galactic Tapestry

Is there life on other planets? This is a very interesting and complex question that has fascinated many people for a long time. The short answer is that we do not know for sure if there is life on other planets, but we have some reasons to believe that it is possible and probable.

One reason to believe there is life on other planets is that the universe is vast and diverse. There are billions of stars and planets in our galaxy and billions of galaxies in the observable universe. Some of these planets may have conditions similar to Earth's, such as the right temperature, atmosphere, and water, which are essential for life as we know it. Is it possible there might be upwards of 40 billion Earth-like planets in our galaxy alone? When you look up in the sky at night and see that blanket of stars, how can there be any doubt that we are not the only Earth?

Another reason to believe that there is life on other planets is that life on Earth is very resilient and adaptable. Life on Earth has survived and thrived in many extreme and harsh environments, such as deep oceans, volcanoes, deserts, and polar regions. Life on Earth has also evolved and diversified into millions of different forms, from bacteria to plants to animals. This suggests that life may also arise and adapt to other planets with different conditions and challenges.

However, some challenges and uncertainties make it difficult to find and confirm life on other planets. One challenge is the distance and time. The closest planets to Earth are located millions of miles away, and the nearest stars are light-years away. This means that it takes a long time and a lot of resources to send and receive signals or probes to explore these planets. Another challenge is the definition and detection of life. We do not have a clear and universal definition of what constitutes life, and we do not have a reliable and sensitive method of detecting life signs, such as biosignatures or techno signatures, from a distance.

Therefore, the answer to the question of whether there is life on other planets is not definitive or conclusive but rather based on probabilities and possibilities. We may never know for sure or discover it sooner than we expect. The search for life on other planets is an ongoing and exciting endeavor that involves many disciplines and technologies, such as astronomy, biology, physics, chemistry, engineering, and artificial intelligence.

Five Original Seeders Of Human Life

According to some sources, the five original seeders of human life on Earth are the Pleiadeans, the Arcturians, the Sirians, the Andromedans, and the Orions. These are star beings who originate from different star systems or galaxies and have contributed to human genetic and cultural diversity. They are also known to be members of the Galactic Federation of Light, a council of enlightened races that seek to promote unity and cooperation within the galaxy and Earth.

Then, there is another interpretation - the five original seeders of human life is a concept that some people use to explain the origin and diversity of human beings. According to this idea, there were five groups of ancient humans who migrated out of Africa and populated different regions of the world, each carrying a distinct genetic and cultural legacy. *These groups are sometimes called the African, Eurasian, Oceanian, American, and Antarctic seeders.*[15]

Neither concept is supported by scientific evidence. Modern genetic and archaeological research shows that human evolution and migration were much more complex and dynamic than a simple model of five seeders can capture. *Humans interbred with other hominid species, such as Neanderthals and Denisovans, and exchanged genes and cultures with each other throughout history.*[16] There is also no evidence that humans ever reached Antarctica before the 19th century.

Therefore, perhaps the thoughts behind the five original seeders of human life are more of a myth than a reality. They may reflect some people's desire to find a simple and neat explanation for human diversity or to justify their beliefs about racial or ethnic superiority or inferiority. The truth is that all humans are part of

---

[15] https://www.smithsonianmag.com/science-nature/essential-timeline-understanding-evolution-homo-sapiens-180976807/

[16] https://www.smithsonianmag.com/science-nature/essential-timeline-understanding-evolution-homo-sapiens-180976807/

one species, Homo sapiens, and share a common ancestry and a common destiny.

Star Being Races/Species

I am in a quandary as to what to call the different races of star beings. We are all one race (Human), but we have many different characteristics that set us apart from one another. Writing about different star being groups can be challenging, as I want to avoid stereotypes, clichés, or offensive terms. After much thought, I offer the following designations and will use bits and pieces of each.

I will use the term **species** to describe the biological classification of the star beings, such as their physical traits, abilities, and origins. This term is more scientific and objective, and it can help you establish the diversity and uniqueness of each star being group.

I will use the term **race** to describe the social and cultural aspects of the star beings, such as their history, beliefs, values, and customs. This term is more human and subjective and can help you explore the conflicts and interactions between different star groups.

I will use the term **kind** to describe star beings' general identity and nature, such as their personality, temperament, and role. This term is vaguer and more flexible, and it can help create a sense of mystery and wonder about the star beings.

As I began researching definitions of the different star beings, I found some of the same information on multiple websites without any citation of resources. Therefore, I will run with much of the information I garnered. At the end of this section, I will list several resources from which I found the most reliable information.

Enigma Of The Cosmos

Some of the prominent star beings that are often mentioned in various sources are:

Pleiadians: They are 9th-dimensional beings who originate from the Pleiades star cluster, also known as the Seven Sisters. They are more human than aliens, with symmetrical features, big blue eyes, and blond hair. They are empathic, nature-loving, and freedom-seeking. It has also been suggested – *"They are* also one of the five original seeders of human life on Earth."[17]

"The Pleiadians, very much, represent our highest potential. Interplanetary peace, unity, and global enlightenment are the potential future of our world, but only if we put all our differences aside and align with the divine within. They are the perfect race to mirror and connect with for human beings since they've already experienced and mastered many of the trials and tribulations we're currently going through as a species.

The Pleiadians have been, like many other races, observing the events on our planet with great concern for our welfare over the last sixty or so years. They've contacted numerous individuals who channel their wisdom and their teachings, which they hope can assist humanity in the expansion of its collective consciousness. Anyone can connect to their vibration and potentially a past or a future self that is living among them in the right state of consciousness.

Pleiadians and the Lyrans are our genetic cousins since they are direct offshoots of some of the highly

---

[17] https://www.annunaki.org/pleiadians-nordic-aliens/

evolved Ancient Orion civilisations. As I mentioned, they represent our highest potential and are the best race to mirror. Most of these beings are blonde and humanoid; they look so remarkably like Scandinavian people that you wouldn't even notice they were ETs if they walked past you on the street, and some do, undercover, observing our planet, lowkey for now."[18]

Arcturians: They originate from the star system Arcturus, the brightest star in the constellation of Boötes. They are highly advanced, both technologically and spiritually. They have iridescent blue skin, elongated fingers, and large eyes. They are benevolent, wise, and compassionate.

According to the beliefs of New Age movements, Arcturians are a very advanced extraterrestrial civilization from the Arcturus star system who wish to share their knowledge and wisdom with Earth's citizens. Some sources claim that Arcturians are 5th—or 6th-dimensional beings, while others say they are 9th—or 10th-dimensional beings.

---

[18] www.reirei.co.uk (Used with permission.)

This question has no definitive answer, as different dimensions may have different meanings and interpretations depending on the perspective and context. However, one thing that seems consistent is that Arcturians have a very high vibrational frequency and a collective consciousness that transcends the limitations of physical reality. They are loving and peaceful, willing to work with any soul that wishes to travel with them to a higher level of consciousness.

According to some sources, the Arcturians have a spoken and written language, which is unlike any human language. Their spoken language is tonal and sounds similar to Chinese or Vietnamese. Their written language is composed of symbols that carry complex meanings and vibrations. They can also communicate telepathically, using light language, a universal language of light. They are also elegant and beautiful, with blue skin and fair hair.

"The Arcturian star is a conscious, living being, like all other stars in the universe. And while there aren't any physical planets orbiting the star, a nonphysical form of consciousness is living within the star itself. Each

of these nonphysical beings are avatars and embodiments of the star's intelligence.

Arcturus is also a gateway into this dimension from the spirit world. Many souls incarnating on planet Earth over the last fifty or so years have come through this gate, and what it does is allow them not to forget as much of their spiritual existence and pre-birth life as most people do when they first incarnate. An example of this would be those who are termed indigo children, those who can clearly remember some of their past lives with astounding accuracy. Another example would be those who aren't as seduced by society and its limiting beliefs as most are; from a young age, they see through the shallow customs of their culture and remain an individual. Many have few friends and find it difficult to connect to others until they find people who accept them as they are, their flaws and all."[19]

Sirians: They are 6th-dimensional beings who originate from the star system Sirius, the brightest star in the night sky. They are diverse, ranging from human-

---

[19] www.reirei.co.uk (used with permission)

like to feline-like to aquatic-like. They are creative, loyal, and adventurous.

"The physical beings living in the Sirius system are amphibious, resembling somewhat of a salamander here on Earth. These are the beings who visited the Dogon tribe in West Africa thousands of years ago. They're not called the Nommo; however, as many believe, they are known as the OUS. When they first arrived on Earth, they introduced themselves to the Dogon Shamans by saying, Nomm-ous, which means "I am OUS." These beings can live in and outside of water and are wise, powerful teachers who are currently sixth density in consciousness. Their home world is mostly water just like the Earth and orbits Sirius B.

Cetacean life is also strongly connected with Sirian consciousness. Those who feel an affinity with dolphins, whales, killer whales, belugas and so on are probably connected to a being that is swimming in the Sirian waters. The nonphysical aspect of Sirius is a super high consciousness that is vibrationally on the same plane as our own higher self. When you connect with this vast, intelligence that lives within the star of Sirius A, your higher mind is infused with wisdom and creative ideas. Since water is a big theme of the Sirius star system, this nonphysical consciousness can also teach you how to live more in alignment with your own higher self, allowing you to flow with the currents of life instead of trying to swim against them as many helplessly do!"[20]

Andromedans: They are 12th-dimensional beings who originate from the Andromeda galaxy, the nearest spiral galaxy to the Milky Way. They are multidimensional, shape-shifting, and telepathic. They are playful, joyful, and curious.

Lyrans: They are 12th-dimensional beings who originate from the Lyra constellation, the oldest and most advanced civilization in the galaxy. They are humanoid, with cat-like features and blue or violet eyes. They are courageous, creative, and passionate.

"Many believe Lyra to be the origin of all life throughout the Milky Way Galaxy; however, it is not true, as I've already said, as the Lyrans are genetically connected to us and the Pleiadians as offshoots of the Ancient Orion bloodlines. Lyra has various forms of life,

---

[20] www.reirei.co.uk (used with permission)

and its star, Vega, has caught the attention of human beings over the last few decades. There are two forms of life in the Vega system: humanoid (although a little taller and paler) and a feline species. These beings work with the Pleiadians and other races which belong to the interstellar community, subtly uplifting the consciousness of undeveloped civilisations through channeLling, storytelling, and mystical experiences.

Those connected to Lyra can channel their wisdom and inspiration through their creative projects. In Astrology, Leo rules the house of creativity, and it's no coincidence that the Lion/Feline race in Lyra is also a very creative species. Tapping into your creative state is the key to accessing the wisdom inherent in this civilisation.[21]

Orions: They are 6th-dimensional beings who originate from the Orion constellation, the most war-torn and chaotic region in the galaxy. They are diverse, ranging from reptilian to humanoid to insectoid. They are ambitious, adventurous, and resilient.

---

[21] www.reirei.co.uk (used with permission)

"Millions of years ago, the Ancient Orion systems were a society under so much pain, darkness, and suppression. The challenges in our current society pale in comparison to the darkness experienced by those incarnated on the Orion worlds back then, (linearly speaking as all lives exist simultaneously in the eternal now).

The Orion souls then moved onto Mars, which also used to be a habitable planet, as NASA has discovered in their recent rover expeditions. Much of the negativity was transmuted there, through more war and turmoil (that's why Mars is correlated with the God of War), but eventually huge asteroids also collided with Mars, wiping out the civilisations there and stripping its atmosphere, that protected its inhabitants from the Sun's radiation.

After jumping to numerous other planets, around 6000 years ago, many of these soul groups incarnated on the Earth, which was seeded with sentient life by other races, hundreds of thousands of years prior. It is no coincidence that what is known as religion and the history being taught in our textbooks in school started around 6000 years ago. Many of those Orion souls and *cultures are currently residing in the Middle East, which has always been a breeding ground for war and mainly over religious beliefs. When the Middle East knows peace, the Earth shall know the peace that passeth all understanding.*[22]

Vegans*:* They are 9th-dimensional beings who originate from the Vega star, the brightest star in the Lyra constellation. They are humanoid, with dark skin and hair and almond-shaped eyes. They are peaceful, harmonious, and musical.

"They are also the founders of the Galactic Federation of Light, a council of enlightened races that seek to promote unity and cooperation in the galaxy."[23]

Grey Matter And Beyond

Greys

Known for their small stature, large heads, almond-shaped eyes, and grey skin, they are highly intelligent, telepathic, and technologically advanced. They are considered to be involved in various genetic

---

[22] www.reirei.co.uk (used with permission)

[23] https://typicallytopical.com/starseed-types/

experiments and abductions of humans, seeking to help humanity evolve, while others are self-serving and manipulative.

Greys, a particular sub-race of Orions, are said to be stuck here reincarnating on Earth life afterlife. This is due to their karma cycle and their interference with Earth beings in a previous past life. They are believed to have traumatized and hurt humans, which galactically means they're stuck here karmically. Contrary to popular belief, the Greys themselves are actually not extraterrestrial beings but a form of mutated human beings from a future, parallel reality.

They represent a reality whereby man almost becomes half machine as they integrate their minds and consciousness with artificial intelligence, so much so that they begin to prioritize the technologies they possess over their natural and organic connection with nature.

They destroyed the forests and the wilderness areas of their world so that it would wind up becoming almost like one large metropolis, but they soon came to realize that their world was fast becoming uninhabitable. They had also tampered with their own genetics to such a degree that they lost the ability to process and feel human emotion, which many of them designated as a lower state of consciousness – preferring the sound reasoning of logic alone. By doing this, however, they stripped themselves of all the facets of the human experience, so much so that they even lost the ability to procreate with each other.

Seeing that their world was on the brink of destruction and their culture was dying, they moved into underground cities where they attempted to clone themselves, but they soon realized that this was also a dead end. The only option these future human beings had was to tunnel back through time into parallel versions of Earth where organic, natural, and human DNA still existed, such as in our time. They met with world leaders and made an agreement that they could swap some of their technologies for permission to abduct people for their genetic material to create their own hybrid civilization, known as the hybrid children.

However, the Greys also encounter a race of highly evolved, psychic, insectoid beings from the Zeta Reticuli system. These beings soon become the overseers of the hybridization agenda as they have the ability to peer into many parallel realities and dimensions simultaneously, helping the Greys ultimately preserve their culture.

They have also warned *this* version of humanity not to go down the same path they went down, to retain their human emotions and their organic connection to nature and the divine. They have assured us that the hybrids they've created will soon come down to be of assistance to mankind in respect to making sure we do not experience the same fate the Greys did many centuries into the future.

Children Of the Cosmos

The Hybrid Children

The hybrid children are a genetic blend of human and extraterrestrial (Zeta Reticuli/Grey) DNA. They are part of a hybridization program that aims to awaken humankind to our infinite expressions and reunite us with our galactic family. The hybrid children are currently living in a different dimension, but they will begin arriving on Earth in the near future. They are very excited to meet their human parents and siblings and to be part of our civilization.[24]

Bashar and his people, the Essasani, are descendants of the hybridization program around 700 years into the future. They share the wisdom of the Sirian beings, who are their mentors, with humanity to prepare us for contact with our own children and the other races that are part of the Interstellar Alliance.

The first race of hybrids who will come down publicly is known as the Yahyel. They will be the first hybrid race to land on the Whitehouse lawn, so to speak, because they look very similar to us, along with the Pleiadians. People who have planets in this lunar mansion are said to be part of the hybridization agenda and have hybrid children of their own, whom they will meet in divine timing.

Everyone involved in the hybridization program, whether he or she remembers here in physical reality, made a soul agreement before coming into this lifetime to take part in the agenda to

---

[24] http://www.hybridchildrencommunity.com/frequently-asked-questions/

awaken humankind to our infinite expressions and reunite us with our galactic family. Five hybrid races were created during the hybridization program, including the Shalinaya/Ya'yl[25] and Essassani civilizations. The Shalinaya ("those who will come first") will be the first to make open contact with Earth. Their ship, known as the *Phoenix Lights*, was seen across Arizona in March of 1997.

Our immediate genetic hybrid children, known as "the freelancers," are hitching a ride with the Shalinaya and are with them on their ships. This group of children is not part of a hybrid civilization . . . they'll be a part of our human civilization! When our immediate human children mix with these hybrids, we will become the 6th hybrid race, galactic humans.

Many parents communicate in dreamtime with their children. Some find themselves shifting dimensions when asleep to aid and assist the

---

[25] www.ishuwa.com

children with lessons they will need to acclimate to our society. [26]

(Personal Note: *While stationed at Eglin Air Force Base in Floria (1996-1999), I worked with some hybrid children and their human families. At that time, I volunteered as a Reiki Master, providing the children with the Reiki energy and balancing their own energies, which ran much higher than our human 3D energies.*

The children were exceptional, and had I not known of their hybrid origins but for looking into their eyes, I would not have known they were different than any other child. I enjoyed my work with the children. Years later, I would find that any specifics I knew about the children, such as where they were located, names, etc., had been erased from my mind.)

Beyond Human

Reticulons

The reticulons are another name for the greys, derived from their star system of origin. The ufologist John Keel

---

[26] http://www.hybridchildrencommunity.com/frequently-asked-questions/

coined the term in his book The *Mothman Prophecies*. He suggested that the greys were not actually aliens but interdimensional beings that could manipulate reality and create illusions. He also speculated that they were behind many paranormal phenomena, such as poltergeists, ghosts, and cryptids.

Reptilians

Reptilians are said to be humanoid reptiles that can shape-shift and infiltrate human society. These insectoid beings are extremely tall – they can be up to nine feet in length. Despite their appearance, they are extremely compassionate beings who are able to communicate telepathically with us and each other.

They also have the ability to see into other dimensions and help others shift to timelines that are more representative of their highest joy.

Many who have contact experiences with the Greys often also see these

Mantis-like beings beside them, often overseeing and observing the interactions that take place.

Reptilians, on the other hand, are also known as a race of humanoid reptiles that are said to inhabit underground bases and infiltrate human society. Reptilians are often associated with conspiracy theories, UFO sightings, and paranormal phenomena.

"Nordics"

According to my web search results, there is a race of aliens called "Nordic aliens" or "Nordics" with features very similar to the Nordic race of humans. They are said to be humanoid extraterrestrials who come from the Pleiades star system and have long blond hair, blue eyes, and fair skin. They have been described as being six to seven feet tall and having telepathic and spiritual abilities.

Some people believe that the Nordic aliens are the same as the angelic beings that are mentioned in many religions and ancient civilizations and that they are here to help humanity evolve and achieve peace and harmony.

Most of their information comes from personal testimonies, anecdotes, or speculation, which may not be reliable or verifiable.

I have barely scratched the surface of the topic of different races, etc. I implore you, the reader, to discover the different races you are interested in and perhaps feel an attachment to them. Those feelings are most likely your own star family and intuition guiding you directly to your star being connections – saving you many hours of research.

CHAPTER 6

Abductions & Implanted Chips

While my intention with this book is to introduce the star beings to you in a positive light rather than the fearful light society has portrayed them in, I would be remiss in my duty if I didn't address the two most talked about negative influences—implants/chips and abductions.

I acknowledge that there have been reports of negative experiences associated with star beings, such as abductions and implants. In all things, I seek to shift my focus to establishing positive and safe communication with star beings. I am offering techniques and practices that readers can utilize to have uplifting experiences.

I believe that purported negative experiences might be misunderstandings, fear-based interactions, or lessons in discernment. It is possible that some star beings might be involved in soul retrieval or energetic balancing, which might feel uncomfortable during the process but ultimately be beneficial. In the context of star-being interactions and soul retrieval, it's important to understand that the concept can be interpreted differently. These are just possible interpretations; I leave it to you, the reader, to discern your own interpretation of a soul retrieval or energetic balancing as it applies to your situation and experience.

Soul Retrieval and the Helping Hand of Star Beings

Some believe star beings play a role in helping individuals retrieve soul fragments or imprints left behind in past lives. The theory suggests that trauma or hardship in past lifetimes can cause energetic blockages or fragments of the soul to become lodged in lower astral planes. Star beings, acting as guides or facilitators, may intervene during dreams, meditations, or even near-death experiences to assist with retrieving these fragments. This process might involve reliving past life experiences to heal the underlying trauma and reintegrate the soul fragments.

While emotionally challenging at times, it is ultimately believed to lead to greater wholeness and healing.

Energetic Realignment & Balancing

This interpretation focuses on star beings helping to balance an individual's energy field. Imagine the human energy field as a complex system with different energetic centers (chakras). Sometimes, these energy centers can become blocked or imbalanced, leading to physical, emotional, or spiritual disharmony.

Star beings, perceived as having advanced knowledge of energy manipulation, could assist in clearing blockages and realigning the energy field to promote optimal health and well-being. This process could involve sensations of tingling, heat, or pressure, which might feel uncomfortable initially but ultimately lead to a more balanced and energized state.

Respecting Your Journey: Consent and Integration

It's crucial to emphasize the importance of individual consent in both interpretations of star being interaction. Soul retrieval or energetic balancing should only proceed if you're open to it and feel comfortable throughout the process. Your free will is paramount.

It's also important to acknowledge that this process might involve reliving past traumas or experiencing unfamiliar energy sensations. These experiences can be emotionally challenging and even frightening. If you choose to undergo soul retrieval or energetic balancing, be prepared for the possibility of encountering these emotions.

Following the process, integration and support become essential. You may need time and guidance to fully integrate the experience and process any emotions that arise.

I hope to equip you with tools to discern authentic communication from negativity. This includes emphasizing the importance of love, light, and positive intentions during communication attempts. Highlight the potential benefits of positive communication with star beings, such as gaining wisdom, guidance, and a deeper connection to the universe.

While some people report negative experiences with star beings, such as abductions or implants, it's important to focus on establishing positive and safe communication. Through techniques like meditation and visualization, we can attract benevolent star beings who can offer guidance and support on our spiritual journeys. Developing discernment to differentiate between genuine communication and negativity is also crucial. When we approach them with love and light, star beings can be powerful allies in our evolution.

The concept of **alien implants** has intrigued audiences for a long time, from the early science fiction trope of weaponized implants in H.G. Wells' *The War of the Worlds* to fueling real-world conspiracy theories about government involvement in extraterrestrial interactions. Science fiction frequently portrays them as tools for mind control, like the Borg in *Star Trek*, or for tracking and communication, as seen in films like *Invasion of the Body Snatchers*.

Ufology adds another layer to the intrigue, with reported cases of alien implants blurring the lines between science fiction and reality.

What Are Alien Implants? Alien implants refer to physical objects allegedly placed inside a person's body after extraterrestrial beings have abducted them. The purpose of these implants ranges from mind control to biotelemetry, allowing you to be tracked for study.

Who Are the Implanters? According to abduction accounts, various star beings or extraterrestrial races are believed to be responsible for these implants. Depending on the narrative, specific races mentioned include Greys, Reptilians, Nordics, and others.

Why Would They Implant Humans? The motivations behind these alleged implants remain speculative: Some believe they serve as tracking devices or communication tools. Others suggest they are part of an experiment or study.

When Did This Phenomenon Begin? Reports of alien implants date back several decades, but they gained prominence during the UFO abduction wave in the 20th century. Researchers and experiencers have documented cases where individuals claim to have had implants removed.

How Are Implants Detected? Detection methods include X-rays, MRI scans, and other imaging techniques. Some implants emit electromagnetic frequencies, adding to the mystery. However, scientific consensus remains elusive due to the lack of rigorous evidence.

Recent Developments: Neuralink and Brain Implants. In a more grounded context, companies like Neuralink (founded by Elon Musk) are working on brain-computer interfaces. Neuralink aims to implant brain chips that allow direct communication between the brain and external devices. While this isn't directly related to alien implants, it highlights our ongoing exploration of merging technology with the human body.

Remember that the topic of alien implants straddles the line between fact and speculation. Skepticism and critical analysis are essential when evaluating such claims. 👽

How To Know If You Have An Implant

Proponents of alien implants claim they can cause various physical symptoms. However, these symptoms are non-specific and could be caused by many underlying medical conditions.

- Unexplained pain or discomfort,

- Unusual lumps or bumps (which could be cysts, lipomas, or other benign growths),
- Metallic taste in the mouth,
- Electronic malfunctions near the implant site (which could be due to coincidence or unrelated technological issues),
- Medical Diagnosis: Standard medical procedures like X-rays, MRIs, or CT scans wouldn't necessarily detect an alien implant, as the materials used might be undetectable with current technology. However, these scans could identify other medical conditions that might explain your symptoms.

If you're experiencing any concerning physical symptoms, it's crucial to consult a doctor to get a proper diagnosis and rule out any underlying medical conditions.

The belief in having an alien implant could be psychosomatic, meaning the symptoms are real but originate in the mind rather than a physical cause. Stress, anxiety, or fascination with alien abduction stories could contribute to these beliefs.

More mundane explanations exist for sensations of something being implanted in your body. These could include:

- A medical procedure you might not remember (such as stitches or minor surgery)
- A foreign object that lodged itself under your skin (like a splinter or piece of jewelry)
- A piercing or tattoo that you forgot about

While alien implants are intriguing, no scientific evidence supports their existence. If you're concerned about something being implanted in your body, it's important to see a doctor to get a proper diagnosis and address any underlying medical conditions. Or is there evidence outside of science? I want to tell you about my experience finding my own implant chip.

Discovering My Own Implanted Chip

In 1994, I experienced what I called the "spins." It didn't matter what I was doing, but what I was looking at would begin to move clockwise through my vision like a movie. I could walk, talk, ride, whatever I might be doing at the time. It was disorientating and intriguing at the same time. As an anthropologist/archaeologist, I looked for the patterns that might trigger it. The only pattern I could find was that it would last exactly 15 minutes, then my vision returned to normal.

I wasn't worried about it per se until one day; it started while I was driving – that didn't work so well. The medical doctors at the Mountain Home Air Force Base, Mountain Home, ID, had no clue. It wasn't vertigo, and they had no explanation. The decision was made to medivac me up to Madigan Army Medical Center, Joint Base Lewis-McChord, Washington, to the medical facility there. I boarded a medivac flight with doctors, nurses, and other patients out of Mt. Home. We almost crashed upon landing at Malmstrom AFB in Montana due to the winds. We took on a couple of patients and flew on to Madigan without incident.

Military friends met me at the air terminal. I stayed with them for the three days I was there. The next day, I went for my appointment. I met several doctors and nurses and carefully noted names and ranks. They appeared as stumped as the Mt. Home doctors; however, here at Madigan, several "hushed and closed-door conversations" took place about my "case."

Ultimately, it was decided that I would return in three weeks for a "sleep study." We drove up to Madigan this time with a horse trailer, as I had purchased a Lipizzaner mare on the first trip when I wasn't at the hospital.

I did the sleep study, and at the end of a very long night and half the morning, I was handed a stack of papers with pictures of all my brain wave activity, etc. I was then scheduled for a "brain stem" study a month later because the sleep study had been "inconclusive," and I could never manufacture a "spin" in front of them so they could study it. I made an appointment before I left the hospital. I had a different set of doctors and nurses for the sleep study.

A week before my "brain stem study" appointment, I called the Medivac office at Mt. Home AFB to schedule my ride to Madigan again as instructed. I gave them my name, appointment information, etc., and they said they would contact me later that day. When they did return my call, they were very hostile, accusing me of trying to use government resources for my benefit (or something similar and stupid). The person said I had never been on a medivac out of Mt. Home to Madigan on the dates provided, that there was no appointment for the brain stem study, nor had I ever been to Madigan as a patient. I supplied all the names of the doctors and nurses I had seen. I gave the names of patients and medical staff on the first Medivac flight and was willing to bring in the stack of papers to prove I had been there.

When I went to retrieve the stack of documents— it was no surprise that they were no longer in the file where I had put them, nor when they called back to inform me that none of the names of the doctors and nurses I had provided had ever worked at Madigan Hospital. The funny thing is that the "spins" had stopped after the sleep study visit. Being me then, it was easy to chalk it up to one of those "strange things that always seemed to happen to me."

It was then I would remember growing up, and my mother had spoken of a time at two years old when "something" happened, and I started "behaving strangely." I can think back to my 2-year-old self now and know she didn't have the words at the time to describe the "spins." I returned to normal within a few weeks, and nothing was thought of as a result of the incident.

You all know the end of this story; I put two and two together this past week while doing a regression and remembered my "spins" incident. I asked if I had a star being, an "alien" chip, and whether or not I had gotten it at two years of age. Of course, the answer was "yes," it had been a malfunction in 1994 that was corrected during my trip to Madigan for my "sleep study." I had been what some have termed "abducted" both times. I am grateful that my memory has allowed me to remember more pieces of my vast "life puzzle."

I asked my spirit guides about the purpose of having a chip and what purpose it held for me. I am a Starseed from the Arcturian star system (I already knew this), and starseeds have chips. Other starseeds may or may not be aware they have a chip. I am researching the purpose(s) of the chip – is it for future contact by our star family? Keeping track of us? Why some and not other starseeds? I was told both my stories (the one I made up and the true one) would be able to help others who may be dealing with a similar situation as mine described above. We are all connected via the web of life.

Perhaps you know you carry a chip; maybe you don't. If you do know, did you make up a story to cover the apparent "abduction" you experienced? Did you find said abduction fearful? Does it bother you to carry a chip, or do you feel it is a reminder of our true "home" (as I do)? Are you willing to share your story with me? If so, please email me at: whenspiritsspeak@yahoo.com

Isn't life exciting? We are spiritual beings who have a physical experience to grow our souls, and we are all connected to the web of life. What happens to one happens to us all. Thank you for allowing me to share "my story."

It would be several years later, when I communicated with my star-being mother, Helena, that I received the answers I was seeking.

Communication with Helena 11/29/2003

J: Greetings Helena.

H: *Yes, my daughter, I am here. You come with urgency this evening?*

J: Yes, as you know, the issue of implants has arisen, and I would like your comment on it if possible.

H: *As you are aware, there was a time when there were many implants implanted into your human race, and as you rightly spoke, it has been by both the Zeta Reticuli and your own government – each for mind control purposes. But just as there is a dark side to implants, so is there a light side. Implants from the light side are alarm clocks for your wake-up calls. They are not obtrusive, and no mind control is attached to them. They are purely for reawaking your higher being to its fuller potential and awareness of so much more than before.*

You wondered after your "spins" experience if you had been implanted. The truth of that matter is "no." You were not implanted at that time; instead, an implant was removed as it had begun to malfunction, and the spins developed. It was members of our own team who removed it from you during your sleep test. They did not remove it, actually, but deactivated it. It had been implanted earlier when you did Reiki on your friend Tim, the walk-in. That was the burning sensation you felt in your arms. As you grew stronger in your own right concerning your communication skills and your strong

110

belief in ALL THAT IS [God, Source], the Zetas were unable to "activate" you. You were then put into a self-destructive mode, which was almost accomplished then. Do you remember it?

J: Vaguely. There was so much I chose to forget about that period of time.

H: *We got you help in a way that was the least suspicious and less hurtful to you at the time. In it all, you got your beautiful mare, did you not? And did you not meet Cele and Tony and learn so much about what else was out there to be involved in interspecies-wise? And you have all the answers to healing and maintaining your own health through James' book – it all came about through that little thing you called the "spins."*

J: It didn't feel "little" when it was occurring, and it was even scarier as the number of occurrences increased. Yet, they maintained their 15-minute run times, and I could never find a trigger for them.

H: *You were so protected, my child, by all of us and* **others that we interrupted their attempts to control you** *through the implant. Thus, the "spins" as we would intercept a transmission and throw everything*

111

off kilter. You wanted to reach us, and yet you thought you were ready, but you were not . . . you still had many questions unanswered to feel comfortable at the time. We were with you and took care of you as best we could, and it was us you felt and saw as you drove home in the blizzard. It was our light that guided you.

J: I'm relieved to know all of this now; I'm sorry I didn't ask sooner. I just knew that they eventually went away, and no one had ever heard of me at Madigan, and the "doctors" who saw me never really worked there. I never put two and two together. Better late than never, they say.

H: *Yes. When the time was right, the teacher came, and we waited for you to come to us.*

J: You know I am ready now to meet you in whatever form you choose, for I have learned acceptance, or at least I think I have.

H: *You have my daughter, and we look forward to the day when we will stand before you.*

J: Then so will I, and I look forward to our meeting. This is not about first contact. I realize it is as much as it is about coming home to my family, who I have been away from for a very long time.

ABDUCTIONS

While abduction experiences are often shrouded in fear, some individuals report a profound transformation following the event. They describe a heightened sense of purpose, a deeper connection to the unknown, or an increased appreciation for life.

Beyond the fear of the unknown, these encounters might represent an attempt at communication or knowledge transfer between civilizations. The motivations behind abductions remain a mystery, but the possibility of interstellar connection offers a fascinating perspective.

Abductions, regardless of their nature, can act as a powerful wake-up call. Confronted with the vastness of the universe and the possibility of extraterrestrial intelligence, individuals may be forced to re-evaluate their beliefs and find new meaning in their lives.

While there are many stories of abductions involving fearful experiences, some individuals report abductions as experiences that led to increased spiritual awareness, healing, or a deeper connection to their purpose. Transformation oftentimes brings about an "awakening experience" rather than a random event.

Stories are common, but what if there are alternative explanations beyond the traditional alien encounter narrative? These could include past life memories surfacing, out-of-body experiences, or encounters with energetic beings, not necessarily physical aliens. Considering these alternative encounters will broaden your perspective and allow you to consider different possibilities.

Depending on the abduction story you read and in spite of the media's attempts to portray the abductees as helpless victims, look for stories where individuals took control of the experience. Examples could include setting boundaries with the beings involved, asking questions, or using protection techniques. This empowers readers and suggests they can have agency even in such situations.

Many abduction stories involve a period of difficulty processing and integrating the experience. Below is a list of books offering resources and techniques readers can use to potentially incorporate challenging experiences into their lives in a positive way. This could involve therapy, support groups, or spiritual practices.

While abduction stories can be frightening, some individuals report them as a catalyst for profound spiritual growth. These experiences might be a form of past life recall, an energetic encounter, or a powerful soul retrieval. It's important to remember that even challenging experiences can hold valuable lessons and opportunities for transformation. By developing our intuition and setting clear boundaries, we can navigate such encounters with empowerment and integrate the wisdom gained into our lives.

Remember, you don't have to dismiss abduction stories. You can create a more balanced and hopeful narrative by offering alternative perspectives and emphasizing the potential for positive outcomes. If you have an abduction story – share it with others in your tribe. Process it for the lessons you learned.

Here are some books already in print that explore past life memories surfacing, out-of-body experiences, or encounters with energetic beings:

Many Lives, Many Masters by Dr. Brian L. Weiss: This classic book explores the concept of past life regression therapy through the cases of patients treated by Dr. Weiss.

Journey of Souls by Michael Newton: This book details the experiences of people who underwent past-life regression therapy under the guidance of hypnotherapist Michael Newton.

Astral Projection by Robert Monroe: This book details the experiences of Robert Monroe, who pioneered methods for achieving out-of-body experiences.

Contact by Carl Sagan: While not explicitly an abduction story, this novel explores the theme of humanity establishing communication with an alien intelligence. The protagonist, Dr. Ellie Arroway, plays a crucial role in deciphering the message and ultimately shapes the nature of the first contact.

A Fire Upon the Deep by Vernor Vinge: This sprawling space opera features the "Zones of Thought," advanced alien entities that can influence reality. The story includes characters who attempt to negotiate with and even manipulate these entities for their own purposes.

Rendezvous with Rama by Arthur C. Clarke: This classic explores humanity's discovery of a mysterious alien cylinder. While there's no direct abduction, the story focuses on scientists trying to understand the purpose of the object and influence its actions.

Communion: A True Story by Whitley Strieber: This controversial book details the author's account of being abducted by aliens. Although its veracity is debated, it touches on themes of setting boundaries and attempting communication with the beings.

When considering non-fiction accounts of abductions, it's important to approach them with a critical eye. These accounts are personal interpretations of often traumatic experiences.

Ultimately, how you process these stories is a personal journey. The experiences may be interpreted as transformative or frightening, but they remain valuable narratives that can offer unique perspectives on the abduction phenomenon.

CHAPTER 7

Starseeds – Star Keepers – Lightworkers

Dolores Cannon (1931 – 2014) was a hypnotherapist and author who explored the concept of starseeds, or souls who have come from other planets or dimensions to help Earth and humanity. She wrote a book called *"The Three Waves of Volunteers and the New Earth,"* describing her findings from her hypnosis sessions with her clients. After many sessions of the same or similar information coming forward, Dolores shared that three generations of starseeds volunteered to come to Earth in three separate waves with a specific mission and purpose.

Much of the following information has been gleaned from research, reading Dolores's books, and visiting the website (Dolorescannon.com). For more in-depth information, I recommend you do your own research; there is plenty out there.

The first wave of volunteers was born in the late 1940s to the early 1960s. They are the pioneers who came to raise the vibration and consciousness of the planet. They have had the hardest time adjusting to life on Earth and often feel alienated, lonely, or misunderstood. They are horrified by the violence and negativity of the world and may have experienced depression or suicidal thoughts. This first group would pave the way for subsequent waves of volunteers.

The second wave of volunteers are those who were born in the late 1960s to the 1980s. They are the antennas that come to channel and transmit energy to the Earth and the people. They have made the transition to life on Earth much easier than the first wave and often work behind the scenes, creating little or no karma. They do not have to do anything; they have to "be." Their energy affects everyone they come into contact with and helps to raise the frequency of the planet. They often prefer to be alone and do not like being around people.[27]

The third wave of volunteers are those who were born in the 1990s to the present. They are the new children who came to show the way and create the new Earth. They are already equipped with enhanced DNA

---

[27] https://Dolorescannon.com

and abilities that are compatible with the higher dimension. They are exceptional, intelligent, and creative. They need challenges and stimulation, not drugs or labels. They are the hope and the future of the world.[28]

Starseeds

I had never heard the term "Starseed" until 2004 when I met Paul, my first mentor, and educator of my starborn lineage and lives. As I understood it, I came to Earth in this lifetime from my Arcturian home to help humanity and the planet evolve to a higher level of consciousness (3rd dimension to 5th dimension).

At a very young age, I wanted to be a healer (that came with my "old soul" mission in this, my last lifetime on Earth). Early in the 1990s, upon meeting my Master Reiki teacher, she encouraged me to learn all I could about alternative medicine and energy healing modalities. As an animal communicator, I began to

---

[28] https://Dolorescannon.com
Starseeds: Psychologists on why some people think they're aliens living on Earth (medicalxpress.com)

teach classes for others wishing to learn to communicate with animals. I slowly began to integrate all of the energy healing modalities I had learned into my classes.

One day, one of my students made the connection – if "I can talk with animals, why can't I talk with others who are in 'spirit.'" A whole new world opened up for my students. Speaking with those who have passed over into the world of spirit is no different than when one prays to one's God. There is no difference at all. Somewhere in time, you just forgot your gift. It has been with you since the day you chose to come into this world. Take the time to remember it now and watch as your world opens up to a whole new dimension—literally.

I got a little off track, but it is important for you, the reader, to understand that communication with other entities, spirits, and God will help to transform this world as humanity searches for a new way of evolving and coexisting with beings from other galaxies.

The question I am most asked when discussing starseeds is: *Do starseeds come from different star systems or races? And how do I know which star system*

I come from? Most starseeds will know their star lineages and missions before choosing this lifetime. While they may come from many different star races, the most common are Pleiadians, Arcturians, Sirians, and Andromedans.

Many Starseeds will tell you they "knew" they were here to assist Mother Earth as she transitions to the "golden age," a time of peace, harmony, and prosperity for all living beings. By using their spiritual gifts and light energy to raise their own vibration and that of others, they seek to create positive change worldwide.

As a first-wave Starseed myself, I can touch my star family using my communication gifts, meditation, dreams, and time travel. Even having that close contact, there is still a loneliness I experience. My greatest gift is when I connect with another starseed. Regardless of the wave we came in on, it is like old-home week. I think our souls recognize each other first. Have you ever felt like you "know" someone, not sure from where or who they might be—chances are, you have just met another Starseed, and believe it or not, we are family.

If you are interested in knowing and exploring your Starseed type and what Star System your soul is from, I have listed on the Resources page several other websites with additional information regarding Starseeds, Star Keepers, and Light Workers.

Star Keepers

Star Keepers is a term used by some New Age movements to describe people connected to the stars and the cosmos. The mission of star keepers is to anchor the light and energy of the Source on Earth. They are often new souls who have never incarnated before but have a direct connection to the Source.

The term "star keepers" can have different meanings, depending on the context. Star Keepers are people connected to the stars and the cosmos, here to assist humanity and Mother Earth ascend to a higher dimension of consciousness and reality.

While similar to the mission, advanced spiritual beings from other star systems that have incarnated to raise Earth's vibration may differ between Star keepers and Starseeds, such as their origin, characteristics, and mission.

- Star Keepers are older, more ancient, and more experienced than Starseeds.
- *They have a specific role in being the record keepers of Earth, whereas Starseeds have different origins and missions depending upon their star system and soul purpose.*[29]

Lightworkers

A Light Worker is a term used to describe a person who feels a strong urge to help others and make the world a better place. Light Workers are often spiritual, empathic, and intuitive. They may have different roles and abilities, such as healing, guiding, teaching, or communicating with other dimensions. They are believed to be part of the Galactic Federation of Light, enlightened beings that seek to promote unity and cooperation in the galaxy.

While researching the concept of Lightworkers, I stumbled upon a Facebook post by Maryanne Gorthouah Ross (April 26, 2024) that resonated deeply

---

[29] https://moonomens.com/starseed-types

with me. It spoke about the "12 Types of Lightworkers" and the idea that we all have unique gifts and talents waiting to be discovered and used for a greater purpose. This piece explores the different Lightworker types. I hope it sparks a fire within you as it did me.

1. *Gridworkers And Gatekeepers*

These are Lightworkers who are working with the grids on Gaia. This could be the human heart grid connecting all awakened humans' hearts. It could be the actual grids on the earth that connect sacred sites through lay lines. It could also be higher energetic grids like the crystalline grid. There is clearing work. Gatekeeping is a more advanced form of grid work in which you work with your team to open interdimensional gates to allow higher levels of light and love.

2. *Divine Lightkeepers*

These are Lightworkers whose core mission (or a huge part of their mission) is to embody the light. They are here to retain a higher vibrational frequency and presence despite whatever is happening in the external.

During tumultuous times and chaotic events, these Lightkeepers consciously focus on embodying the light and expanding it beyond them to neutralize challenges and density. They uplift humanity and support us all in the unfolding awakening process.

3. *Transmuter*

Transmuters dive into the negativity in order to transmute it and release it into the light. This returns the negativity to divine neutrality, returning it to presence and balance. Transmuters may be working on behalf of the collective consciousness and all humanity by transmuting past karma. There are also a lot of Lightworkers who are transmuting along their ancestral lines. You may have chosen to be born into an ancestral line with a lot of negative karma so that you can release, dissolve, heal, and help your entire ancestral line level up vibrationally. Which in turn helps all of humanity.

4. *Healers*

Healers serve humanity, the earth, animals, all souls, and all beings. Healing can take so many different forms. It can be mental, emotional, physical, or spiritual. There are so many different modalities. If you are a Healer, listen to your internal guidance about the modalities, techniques, and ways you can serve through your gift. The work of healing as a Lightworker also includes yourself. You're raising your vibration and filling yourself up with light so you can then heal, support, serve, love, and guide others.

5. Seers, Psychics, Clairvoyants

These are Lightworkers who have opened their third eye or their psychic sight to see beyond the physical, beyond the veil of illusion. This gift can take many forms. You can provide readings or services to inspire, empower, and help guide others. You can also look for areas where healing, transmutation, or release are needed and focus your energy there. This is where your light, power, and presence can most make a difference.

6. Divine Blueprint Holders

We all have a unique divine blueprint, a template for our fully awakened self. All Lightworkers have this template, but the Divine Blueprint Holders are actively tuning into it and retrieving the codes of awakening that are unique to them. This way, they embody their codes and send them forth through the crystalline grid, the human heart grid, through service or love in any form.

The Divine Blueprint Holders are tuning in to their fully awakened being and shining this forth. This gift also includes the divine blueprint for the awakened earth and humanity. Tune into this awakened template and call it forth to bring ascension into the present moment, right here and now.

7. Dreamers

Dreaming, transmuting through dreams, interdimensional travel, and going into the dream space all allow you to access alternate dimensions of experience. Dreamtime is real, so pay attention! What are the symbols in your dreams? Write them down. Meditate on them. Every time you remember a dream, take time to ponder it and take some truth away.

What could the higher dimensional manifestation of that dream be? If you dream that you are going to school, the higher dimensional correlation means that you are, in your dreamtime, studying and leveling up. You're taking on new skills and gifts as a soul so that you can be of more service. There is so much light work that happens during dreamtime.

Before you go to sleep, set the intention to do light work and connect with your higher self. Ask your angels to reveal to you what you need to know, and then pay attention! Dreaming is an incredible opportunity to grow and learn.

8. Messengers

A Lightworker who is receiving guidance and messages from the Divine, Angels, Ascended Masters, Galactics, and your higher self is a Messenger. Share these messages through videos, blogging, teaching, or writing. Whatever the media, whatever the form, Messengers receive guidance from Spirit and pass it on in order to serve humanity and the awakening process.

9. Divine Blueprint Creators And Manifesters

These are the Lightworkers who are actively involved in weaving light in order to manifest positive changes on the earth. This could come in the form of intending and manifesting positive timelines.

It could come in the form of manifesting positive events or creating the template for greater love, greater light, or harmonious co-creation. Divine Blueprint Creators manifest not only for self-interest and self-gain but also for the highest interest of all beings, Gaia, animals, and all of humanity. This is manifestation in its highest form. These Lightworkers manifest collectively for the highest interest of all. This is powerful.

10. Ascension Guides

These are people who are ascending. They are stepping into greater light levels and sharing what they learn about the ascension process.

They show us how to overcome some of the pitfalls and tune into the blessings to help everyone who has the opportunity to ascend.

11. Wayshowers

Wayshowers are lightworkers who walk their walk. They are showing the way! Perhaps they aren't consciously teaching as Ascension Guides are, but rather embodying the ascension process and living in their highest authenticity. They live awakened, inspired lives, keeping the highest interest of all beings in mind.

12. Unifiers

These Lightworkers see how everything connects with everything else. They are good at finding patterns and merging various philosophies into one. They are translators who gather the teachings of other Lightworkers, the truths and philosophies of spiritual masters, and straightforwardly shape them for people to consume. The Unifiers are good at perceiving the essence behind different opinions. That's how they can find ways to connect people together. They naturally see beyond the two sides and understand the whole that the two sides are a part of.[30]

Starseeds And Earth Angels

There is not a clear-cut difference between an Earth Angel and a Starseed, as they are both terms that describe souls who have incarnated on Earth to help humanity and the planet. However, some people may use these terms to emphasize different aspects of their origin, mission, or connection.

An Earth Angel is a soul with a strong connection to the angelic realm, while a Starseed is a soul with a deep connection to the stars and other planets and may

---

[30] Maryanne Gorthouah Ross, "The 12 Types of Lightworkers," Facebook post, April 26, 2024.

have lived as a star being before coming to Earth. Bringing their star family's wisdom, knowledge, and light to Earth, they endeavor to help humanity and the planet ascend and evolve.

Earth Angels and Starseeds are lightworkers, meaning they are here to shine their light and raise the world's vibration. They may have highly sensitive, intuitive, empathic, creative, and spiritual traits. They may also face similar challenges, such as feeling different, lonely, misunderstood, or homesick. They may have a strong sense of purpose but also struggle with finding their true path or fitting in with society.

However, Earth Angels and Starseeds may also have unique characteristics, depending on their soul history and expression. For example, an Earth Angel may have a more gentle, nurturing, and angelic energy, while a Starseed may have a more adventurous, curious, and cosmic energy. An Earth Angel may be more drawn to working with the angels, nature, and animals, while a Starseed may be more drawn to working with the star beings, technology, and science. An Earth Angel may have more memories or dreams of the angelic realm, while a Starseed may have more memories or dreams of their star home.

Ultimately, Earth Angels and Starseeds are not mutually exclusive categories, and one can identify with both or neither. The most important thing is to recognize and honor one's own soul essence and to follow one's own guidance and intuition. Whether one is an Earth Angel, a Starseed, or something else, the common goal is to serve the highest good of all. 🙏

Indigo, Rainbow, And Crystal Star Children

I would be remiss if I didn't speak about the Star Children, known as the Indigo, Rainbow, and Crystal Children. Indigo, Rainbow, and Crystal children are starseeds or souls from other planets or dimensions and help Earth and humanity. They are often born with enhanced abilities like intuition, creativity, and empathy. They have different characteristics and missions, depending on when they were born and what they came to do. My daughter is an Indigo child. Like me, she knew she was different the day she was born, and so did I. I prayed night and day to understand how to deal with and teach her and to know the things she would need to survive in this lifetime.

Indigo Children are the older generation, born in the 1960s-1980s. They are the rebels, the system-busters, the truth-seekers. They came to challenge the old paradigms, expose the corruption, and awaken the masses. They are often strong-willed, independent, and outspoken, having difficulty fitting in, following rules, and accepting authority.

Crystal Children are the middle generation, born in the 1980s-1990s. They are the healers, the peacemakers, and the unifiers. They came to bring harmony, joy, and love to the world. They are often gentle, compassionate, and optimistic. They have an uncanny connection to nature, animals, and other dimensions.

Rainbow Children are the newer generation, born in the 1990s-present. They are the innovators, the leaders, the creators. They came to show the way and create the new Earth. They are often exceptional, intelligent, and creative. They need challenges and stimulation, not drugs or labels. Like the Third Wave, they are the future of the world.

The main differences and similarities between indigo, rainbow, crystal children, starseeds, star keepers, and lightworkers are souls who have come from other planets or dimensions to help Earth and humanity.

They are all born with enhanced abilities like intuition, creativity, and empathy, and they have a sense of mission and purpose. They may have different roles and abilities, such as healing, guiding, teaching, or communicating with other dimensions.

Starseeds, Lightworkers, and Star Children: Challenges and Opportunities

Starseeds, lightworkers, and star children are individuals who feel a deep connection to the cosmos and a burning desire to uplift humanity and the planet. However, their journeys on Earth aren't without hurdles. Feelings of alienation, loneliness, and a sense of being misunderstood by those who don't share their perspective or vibrational frequency can be common. The density, duality, and negativity of the 3D world can also present challenges in adapting to this reality.

Additionally, they may face resistance, opposition, or even persecution from those threatened by their light and message. Balancing spiritual and material needs, finding their place in the world, navigating careers and relationships—these can all be areas of struggle. The wounds, traumas, and karma carried from past lives or other dimensions can add another layer of complexity. Furthermore, the ascension process itself can be intense, bringing forth a range of physical, emotional, mental, and spiritual changes and symptoms.

Despite the challenges, immense opportunities await these individuals. Finding their soul family, a tribe or community of like-minded and like-hearted people who provide support and inspiration, is a powerful gift. Discovering and expressing their unique gifts, talents, and passions can bring joy and fulfillment to themselves and those around them.

Earth's rich tapestry of cultures, perspectives, and experiences offers invaluable lessons and growth. These beings have the potential to contribute significantly to the collective awakening and transformation of humanity and the planet by radiating love, light, and wisdom. Connecting and collaborating with star beings, guides, and allies from other dimensions adds another layer of support and guidance to their journey.

Ultimately, they can also embrace the beauty and abundance life on Earth has to offer, finding joy in nature, animals, and the arts. It's important to remember that these are just general challenges and opportunities, and each individual's journey and purpose will have its own unique variations and exceptions.

Healing and Energy Work: Starseeds and lightworkers bring forth powerful healing energies to support physical, emotional, and spiritual well-being. Alternative healing modalities such as Reiki, crystals, sound, or meditation can transfer energies to others.

Teaching and Guidance: Starseeds and lightworkers share spiritual knowledge, wisdom, and guidance to help others on their spiritual journey. They may use various platforms, such as books, blogs, podcasts, or social media, to reach and inspire their audience. Often, you will find them offering services such as personal coaching, mentoring, or counseling to those seeking assistance.

Activism and Service: Starseeds and lightworkers are passionate about improving the world. They may engage in various forms of activism and service, such as volunteering, donating, campaigning, or protesting, to support causes that align with their values and vision. Their gifts and talents create positive change in their communities and across the globe.

These are some of the general roles and contributions of starseeds and lightworkers, but of course, there may be variations and exceptions depending on each individual's journey and purpose.

And just when I thought I was done, I ran into a mention of *"Angel Starseeds."* Most information on *Angel Starseeds* comes from the website www.angelfairyhealing.com. There is a lot of information to process, and this is the first time I have heard of Angel Starseeds, so it is new for me as well.

Angel Starseeds: Messengers of Light

Angel Starseeds are a unique breed of Lightworkers, their souls hailing from the angelic realm. Driven by a mission to illuminate the world and uplift humanity, they possess several distinct characteristics. Angel Starseeds are naturally drawn to energy healing, finding solace and guidance in angelic energy and communication with their celestial guides. Often highly clairvoyant, they possess a well-developed third eye, granting them access to visions and intuitive insights. Though they may have suppressed their powerful manifesting abilities to blend in, these gifts hold immense potential.

Angel Starseeds radiate an inner light that draws others in, fostering feelings of peace and love. Their deep longing is to find a kindred spirit family, a community that resonates with their unique abilities and understands them on a deeper level. Naturally drawn to peaceful environments, Angel Starseeds find solace and inspiration in the company of gentle souls, calming music, artistic expression, the beauty of nature, and the love of animals.

CHAPTER 8

My Own Involvement with Star Beings

Throughout my life, I've had occasional yet profound communication experiences – with beings beyond our world. They were private and deeply personal, a secret I kept close. In 2002, moving to Cannon Air Force Base in New Mexico brought me into a community of like-minded individuals of Starseeds and Lightworkers. This newfound connection sparked the recording of these past encounters.

These dialogues weren't structured interviews but free-flowing exchanges. My questions, and those of a few close friends, intertwined with the messages received. This book presents the most relevant of these communications chronologically. I hope to share valuable insights about our shared origin among the stars and the loving presence of our star families.

This journey began with self-discovery, and as my understanding of my own star lineage grew, missing pieces of my life fell into place. Perhaps you, too, feel a sense of displacement. Embrace the possibility that you might also be a Starseed awakening. Many are, as the need for lightworkers grows in preparation for a new era – a world of peace and unity.

Join me as we explore these communications and the potential for connection with both our star family and those who have transitioned within our Earth family.

Conversations interspersed throughout this book were recorded from 2003 to the present. I will only use bits and pieces of most conversations as directed!

2003

Communication with Helena Cmdr. Starship Capricorn, 12/31/03

Helena: . . . *You and I have our own personal relationship, and it is different than that I share with others. We have spoken of this before. It will always be that way. We must keep the enthusiasm up with the others as we need friends in many places. While it is our desire not to come "in force," it is a reality that, at this time, we must do so for our own protection purposes. If there is any criticism, and I don't mean this in a negative way – you, too, go through life just knowing it is there and will happen. Do you go out at night and look to the skies for us? Do you take everything for granted that it will happen, and you will deal with it when it does?*

Shakana: Yes, I guess I do now that you mention it. I know you are real, I know you are there in the skies, and I know you will come soon. I will be ready when that happens. Is that wrong?

H: *No, that is not wrong. It is a "knowing," as you call it, and you are comfortable with that knowing. Because you have been through the "excitement period" before and have now settled into this comfortable rocker of knowing, this all seems frivolous to you. My child, we must allow the others to have their time of excitement, must we not?*

S: Yes, I guess so. I have always erred on the side of caution, yet I don't want to be so cautious that I miss out on things. I want to write your book, but I want to do it when I have time to just sit and do nothing else. Right now, I really want to finish those projects. I get really "hung up" when I commit to doing something at this time for this long each day. I'm attempting to escape being "routine" oriented and driven. We will get it written. I need an extra ounce of inspiration – an idea that won't leave my head and keeps itself in the front of my mind – it is then that I come to the computer and begin writing and not stop until it is finished. That is what I am waiting for. As it is now, I have a million interruptions and want the time for it to flow freely.

H: *And when do you think that time will be?*

S: One day soon. Perhaps I could write all night if I got a second wind at night. Early mornings are fine after I feed, get my coffee, let the dog in and out, etc.

H: *We will work on it soon. Go into your day and finish the project you have worked so diligently on, and we will talk soon. Murko sends his love and best wishes for a healthy and prosperous New Year.*

S: And I, in return, send my love to him; I want so much to be with him, and soon we will be. Looking forward to seeing you soon, my mother.

H: *My love to you, daughter of mine. In you, I am proud.*

S: Thank you. I understand the need to get this book written as quickly as possible. Each day, I see more of our freedoms slipping away, and I hear your coming is imminent. To see you again in the flesh would be amazing. It has been so long since I have felt a hug from those who love me.

H: *Yes, and we have much to share with you. Your father is ill, and I worry his days are numbered. While we do not age as you humans, and our bodies are engineered differently than humans, there are times when the shell is no longer viable.*

S: Arturus and Lord Ashtar were both my fathers. One by birth, one out of love.

H: *Arturus, his flame burns rather low these days. He will not give up until he reunites with you again. There are so many things he longs to share with you. There are so many words left unsaid: words of power, words of love, words of positivity, and words of hate.*

S: Then I hope I will be there when that time comes. I have sent my dis-ease back to my past lives from whence they originated. My body feels much better now. I believe I am healed in this lifetime of all that came before. I didn't realize there could be such a pull from a past life. Then again, without it, I would not be remembering my starborn life today with such familiarity.

H: *There is much for you to remember, and it will come in small doses as you prepare to take on your new role. You have friends who are awakening, and they will all be connecting with one another soon. Your star galaxy village is materializing. You will not be required to do this alone; we are here for you and will continue to watch and be part of each meeting.*

144

S: So, where do we go from here? I am doing my best to find the time to do the communications and everything else. I need quiet times carved out to meet with everyone without interruptions, which are not always easy to come by.

H: *We do understand and will work within your timeframe.*

S: If something happens to Father before we meet again, will you call me back long enough to say goodbye?

H: *Not to say goodbye, my child; there is no such thing as "goodbye," nor do we go anywhere "out there." We simply cease to exist. Our bodies become stardust, and we once again become the stardust that built our planet and many planets. Our creator god used stardust to fashion humans, called "man." No matter how many lifetimes you live through, stardust is in your DNA and is a part of who and what you are. We are all "one," and we are forever connected.*

Gorto: *Many messages are being spread through our systems. We are all reaching out and hoping to connect and share our warnings and invitations with you humans. Time is of the essence. You cannot wait any longer to tell our stories. There are so many to tell.*

S: I will do my best to meet with you each night and write your words. I, too, am anxious to get started, as it brings me closer to "home."

H: *You are welcome here anytime you choose to come. There is always room on this starship for you. We would welcome your laughter, for our days are oftentimes spent boring one another here.*

S: Are you asking me to return to my "as if" life? I was there so many years ago, living in my "as-if" world day after day. It felt good to be home, and I enjoyed catching up with old friends (really old friends). But then, at the end of the day, I had to return to my real world, which was very depressing. Returning to the lower energies took its toll on my own psyche, and I could no longer manage it. I wasn't as strong then as I am now. Disease and a wish to die will change you, as it did me.

H: *We know; we stood back and watched. It wasn't easy watching you struggle and not stepping in, but it was for your own good- the decision to live had to be your own. We realized it could have gone either way. We were grateful the spirit children and your soldier Johnny Blue were able to reach you; you were so far gone. But we couldn't, wouldn't interfere, even with the risk of losing you. We had to stand back and watch. We whispered for you to remember who you were and where you came from. We clapped for you when you finally came out of the mists and spoke with Johnny. We knew you would live then. You had a rough road ahead, but you had something to live for. Your star was not ready to burn out yet.*

S: There is so much catching up for us to do. So little time . . .

❊ ❊ ❊

Over the years, I've had a few profound experiences that have shed light on my place in the universe. While these communications with beings from beyond our world weren't frequent, they left a lasting impact. I felt compelled to record these experiences, and after careful consideration, I've decided to share a couple of the most significant ones with you.

What makes these encounters so compelling is the way they resonated with my life's journey. The insights they provided about my purpose in this particular lifetime have unfolded with surprising accuracy.

These communications were recorded and then filed away, never to be seen again until I pulled them out and dusted them off to share with you, my readers.

Communication 07/21/2003 –
This is a communication I held with my "team," my "assistants," and my "spirit guides."

Shakana: Dearest Team, I came this morning in response to a writing I must do for tomorrow. I ask for your assistance in defining myself so that I will be understood.

Team: *Our help is offered, dear one, as you struggle to define a concept that is foreign to many yet so familiar to those who are of your heritage. Your starborn heritage of long ago past. So, let us begin there. You are a child of All That Is, a soul of the most high. You recognize your powers to be as he/she is, and forever more shall be. You have forgotten some of that royal birth in this lifetime and struggle now to regain and recognize what that entails; you seek to find the "missing pieces" and have turned your search within and without.*

You have learned of your past life on Atlantis and seek now to understand how that can be while knowing in your heart that it was so. Atlantians were a mighty

148

culture that rivaled the Egyptians. Still, bringing about their demise was necessary, keeping their secrets hidden until a future generation would be ready for them and continuing where we left off. While it was a traumatic death for all, it was necessary so that our Island would sink and not be found. It was with great pain and heartbreak that this task was accomplished.

We then turned our attention to assisting the Egyptian race so that while the secrets were hidden, advancement could continue. If your culture, scientists, and archaeologists understood the brilliance behind the pyramids and their architecture, they would not question the teachings as they do now. But as you know, ego stepped in and rode a very tall horse. Ego will take a fall soon and come crashing down, and those like you who have always held the secrets of Atlantis deep within your soul will bring forth the message of your/our beginnings.

Yes, we assisted the Toltecs and the Anasazi, and great information to all who followed. The pyramids were just the beginning of all that could be if your cultures had allowed our information to flow forth. You, dear one, hold many secrets of the past, and when the time is right, and your culture is ready, you will speak forth your truth for all to hear. Your past lives have been in preparation for all that you have carried forth and will one day present. We have seen your strength and passion for equality for all. Your most memorable lifetimes are those you remember with fondness and those from which you learned great wisdom. They are all coming together in this lifetime, and much needs to be done.

You have begun the process and run into obstacles along the way – though we do not see them as obstacles as you see them. They have shut you down on many occasions, and we have waited patiently for "you" to return to your search so that we can assist you in your discovery. So here we are today to tell you much of what you already know, some of which you have already guessed, and much more to come.

As you know, you were born Quantarus of Atlantis and studied hard to learn all that was presented to you. You were quick in your grasp of the knowledge being presented to you. But most of all, you always sought fairness in any decision you offered. You were strong in spirit, stood your ground, and told your truth regardless of the consequences. As you know, people shied away from the truth, not wanting to hear it many times.

Your life was a struggle in that sense, and your frustration grew. You continually questioned, "Why someone would not want to hear the truth." You were imprisoned for your outspokenness, and you languished there for many years. But not one to let a minute pass without some learning benefit to be had, you taught those in prison with you – ever the teacher.

Your wisdom was sought as many sorted through their own lives in search of a greater understanding of their purpose on this earth. Many went back into the world a better person for your teachings and made a difference in the lives of others.

Your time was short as you were called back for a greater mission. Never fear that you won't be remembered. You made a difference.

In this lifetime, you chose your parents in hopes that they would bring forth opportunities for you to again make a difference. Unfortunately, that didn't happen in the way you had planned, and you have struggled every day since then, always knowing there was something more but not knowing what that "something" was. Your desire to make a difference has been strong throughout this lifetime, though you didn't always notice it. You sought "to be different" instead. Events you experienced afforded you that opportunity.

But in that being "different," you encountered much resistance in the physical forms of rejection and lack of recognition. It wasn't until you learned you were "Quantarus" that you stood tall again and remembered your inner strength. You would not have met with such resistance if you had chosen another path into the educational side of alternative medicines and healing.

You chose, however, to be different in the military and conventional scientific groups, and your ideas have been thrown back at you on numerous occasions. Your ideas are not "wrong," my child. Your ideas are the truth and the wisdom that you know and hold sacred in your soul, but you will struggle to get people to believe them for themselves. The harder you struggle, the more rejected and unrecognized that you feel. It is time for you to speak your truth and let it fall where it may.

Some are ready for it, and some are not; that is not something you can change. Each must find it within themselves. It must be their own decision to believe, for they will only discover their own truths within their soul.

Yes, your ideas are taken and used by others who profit from them, but that is only in this physical lifetime,

"All That Is" knows the source of their information, for you are one of his/her most trusted messengers. While you aren't seeing it directly at this time, you have made a difference, and you will continue to make a difference as you ask questions and cause those who ride those tall horses to rethink what they believe. And though you may never be told you made a difference in their life, you will see it one day soon. When you hear your words coming back to you from someone, you may know that you have made a difference.

You have helped many and will continue to help many as you travel forth in search of Who you Are. This is a never-ending journey, as there is always much to discover. Some who never seek or ask the question must continue to return until that spark is ignited from within. We are pleased with all you have done, and as you look forward to your work with Shanti as she travels into Shambala, we will assist you. You have the knowledge, power, and strength to bring this information forth, as you were chosen for this mission long ago. Never believe you haven't made a difference, for you have and will continue to do so. Go forth in peace and love from your family here, there, and everywhere.

S: I would ask to whom on my team I am speaking, as you sound as if you are of Starborn lineage yourself and know quite a bit about me.

T: *I am, I am Lord Sanctus. I have come forth at the request of your team to offer this information to you. These stories can be passed down from father to daughter in any lifetime. I have spoken here of only three lifetimes, but you have lived so many more, and as you are ready, you will begin processing them all. It is important for you to know each one, but only as you are ready for that information. My appreciation to your team for all that they have assisted you in achieving.*

I am proud of you, my first child and we will speak at another time about your mother's love for you and your life. I have followed your progress through your soul's development and have always been proud.

I realize you have not felt that from your Earth family. Things did go amiss in that regard, but it made you a stronger person for it. You began to question everything from an early age and continue to question it today. Never stop asking the questions, for there are many answers waiting to be heard. And always remember your truths. (Lord Sanctus was my father in one of several starborn lifetimes).

S: Wow, I am honored by your presence and grateful for the information you have provided. A few more missing pieces of my puzzle were solved. I thank you.

❊ ❊ ❊

It would take a few years before I would be ready to talk about my Earth father. But one day, I did in a communication with my star being mother, Helena.

Communication with Helena 11/29/03 7:41 pm

Helena: . . . *Just as you took a leave to come to earth, so did he work on the test pilot projects of your jets to break the sound barrier. It was vital for us to have that information, and so he volunteered to gather it for us. His death was not of your doing; it was determined long before you were even born. And all those who died in the crash that day were a part of our crew and are here with us now. Nothing is ever in vain. It was not your words of*

155

anger that brought the plane down. They felt no pain as
their spirits left long before the plane hit the mountain.

Jeri: And was the sheepherder on the ground in on it?

H: *No, that was unfortunate. He had been warned not to*
go where he was at the time. He did not listen and paid
the consequences. But his spirit joined our crew as they
came forth, and he is here with us now.

J: Wow! There is so much more information than I
expected or even hoped for. Why has my father not
contacted me before this?

H: *That is something you and he must discuss. You were*
pretty angry at him for leaving you that day. You knew
he wasn't coming back, and yet you didn't understand
at that age that there was nothing that you could do to
prevent him from leaving.

J: Sometimes, not knowing the truth is harder than
knowing it. I felt guilty for having said the angry words
as a 10-year-old that, in my mind, had caused my
father's plane to crash, killing five other people. The
truth was always right in front of me; I just forgot to
ask.
    I was able to obtain the official US Navy Accident
Report via FOIA (Freedom of Information Act) once it

had been declassified in 2011. My father had not caused or been responsible for the crash, even though he had been the navigator at the time. What I didn't know beforehand but had suspected all along was that he had been thrown from the plane at the time of the crash and was the only body not burned.

They knew the time of the crash because his watch stopped when he impacted the ground. I could never visualize him as burned, no matter how hard I tried, and my mother refused to tell me if I was correct because she feared my ability to see beyond the veil. I knew his spirit had lived on.

2004

Communication 012904 with Helena

Shakana: Greetings, my mother. It's another beautiful morning on planet Earth. I anxiously await your arrival so that I can share its many wonders with you. I cannot imagine living solely on a starship and not having the pleasure of touching the earth. I guess, now knowing some of my past life history as a starborn, there was a time when I lived such as that. I just don't remember yet. Okay, now I am comfortable and can begin in earnest.

Helena: *I too long for a return to our planet to again touch solid ground, but after all these years, living in a starship has become that "earth" that "ground" we have chambers to which we can go and experience your seasons as you experience them. I love springtime when everything is green, fresh, and in bloom.*

S: My favorite is fall and winter, at least at the beginning. When the air turns crisp, there is a chill in the offering when all seems much brighter as it prepares for its winter nap. The first snowflakes of winter as they cover the ground and turn everything magical and twinkly (not sure that is a real word, but it is my word) when the sun's first rays hit it. The moon in the fall always seems so much bigger and right there in front of you. The harvest moon has to be my favorite – big and yellow, casting enough light to plant by, but we don't grow in the fall, so I don't understand why. I just got it – "harvest moon" – when the last of the crops are harvested, and the crops and the fields are put to rest. You'd think I was a blonde this morning.

H: *My daughter, we know you are not blond . . .*

S: Did I have hair as a starborn?

H: *Oh my yes, and plenty of it – bright red hair. Long and beautiful.*

S: It has changed now. There are still red tints with dishwater blond highlights.

Communication with my earth father from this lifetime, now known as Commander Korton of the Starship Capricorn, 01/21/04

Shakana: Helena, may I speak with my father?

Father: *I am here, daughter; you have grown into a beautiful woman.*

S: More like you than you know.

F: *I can see that. You took on my spirit of adventure and legalism, did you not?*

S: The legalism part—duality, black and white—was truly a world without color. I am attempting to add color by freeing myself of self-imposed constraints.

Father, why did it take so long for me to find out the truth about your passing? Why did you let me go for so many years believing it was my fault, my angry words that killed you?

F: *It was a guilt you carried buried deep within, and until you were ready to bring it to the surface, there was no way for me to approach it. Your understanding of death at that time was finality. It wasn't until you were ready to listen that you knew it was a lie you had been led to believe; only then were you ready to search for new answers to fill the void of the old answers you knew not to be true.*

S: Why does mom refuse to believe the truth?

159

F: *Your mother always wanted to see the good in people. She never dwelt on the bad. Her repressed anger left her bitter but only brought her to a place of believing what she was told.*

S: She has come into her own money-wise, but it seems there will be a few years left to enjoy it. Why do we go through life working all those years, scrapping by, only to inherit money at the end when we are too old to enjoy it?

Why couldn't we start with a large amount and live our lives at the beginning?

F: *Because by the time you get to the end, there will be none left, and you would then struggle as you did at the beginning of your life.*

S: My point exactly.

F: *You have all the wealth you need, my daughter. It is inside of you, and it costs nothing to give away. The more you give away, the more you receive in return, and your well will overflow. There is much in your future to enjoy; learn to let go and enjoy it. You are creative and talented, and your work is valuable. Go now and use your talents well. Find your passion, and all else will disappear.*

S: I truly miss you and am so sorry for our angry words.

F: *As am I—it is water under the bridge now – go forth and multiply all you have been given – pass it on.*

S: Thank you. I love you; I truly do.

F: *We will be together soon enough; you can show it to me then. In the meantime, I am here; reach out and touch me.*

S: So you went from jet planes to spacecraft; I bet those astronauts you used to train with would envy you now! You made it to the big time, and they are still stuck here on Earth with only memories and longings of where you are now.

F: *Yes, in the end, it all works out as it was meant to be.*

2010

I learned of my star being half-brother Lysanias early in 2008. One day, an email came through, and he introduced himself. Yes, I knew of his earth name at the time, I just had not heard the story of our connection and how it all came about. In this lifetime, he struggled, and I knew he would be leaving soon. Because we resided several states apart, I could never meet him physically. One day, the emails stopped coming, and I knew he was getting ready to transition. I contacted Helena as I knew she would know what was going on and share it with me even though she had not raised him.

Communication with Ashtar and Helena
02/23/2010

Shakana: Good morning, Mother and Dad. Has Lysansis come aboard yet?

Helena: *Shortly, daughter for it is almost finished.*

S: I am sad to hear that, even though I have never met him face to face during this lifetime. He is still my brother. I know he has struggled this past year; perhaps it is time. I have learned much from him these past few months.

H: *You aren't ready yet to take on all that he was doing on Earth; we know you will be there when the time comes to greet us.*

S: Yes, that is a given. I don't know what honored me, but I am so grateful to take it. I just feel that if I can get all the other stuff done away with and become less

162

cluttered and overwhelmed, then I could devote more time to all the things you would have me do.

H: *We know that, daughter, and are willing to wait, but you must make an effort each day to move forward and get all of that done. Sitting in your chair all day, hour after hour, is not getting anything done except more sitting in your chair.*

S: You are correct, mother. I do a lot of that. I just get overwhelmed each time I think of doing something to reorganize my life. I needed to double myself to have a friend with whom I could work and talk, and I knew it would go much quicker.

H: *You always want someone other than yourself. Do you not understand that there is only yourself? You are it! You have everything necessary to get it done and provide the answers, and everything is within YOU.*

S: True, that is what my brother desperately tried to tell me all along. I'm the only one I need. I have all the answers. My higher self has all the answers. Why did it take so long to figure that out?

H: *Some just take longer than others. Accepting information from others has never been your strong suit without first ensuring it is correct. We hear you ask and then question all that you receive – why ask in the first place if all you are going to do is question?*

S: I have no clue. It must be a trust issue thing. I trust no one, not even myself, and hence look outside of myself for what I desire. All the while knowing that the answers lie within. They always have and always will.

H: *We see that. Futile search so far, hasn't it been?*

S: Of course. Time consuming and useless in the end.

H: *Can you imagine how your life could be if you were to get rid of all the unnecessary clutter and just deal with what you need now? Do you realize how freeing that could   be?*

S: Perhaps that is what I fear—being free, for it leaves no room for an excuse to stay.

H: *Very true. Being free allows you to move on.*

S: So I'm afraid of moving on?

H: *That is how we see it. Even with your debt paid and free of clutter, you will stay.*

S: I will stay until I can find great homes for the animals, especially the horses. Or find a way to take them with me. I owe them that, and I have promised them I want it no other way. I won't go back on my promise to them.

H: *You are doing fine, daughter, and we watch over you, as does your earth father. You must come to visit sometime and let us sit and chat. You are welcome aboard any time.*

S: Sounds so casual, Mother.

H: *We all can change when it is called for.*

S: Yes, we can. My love to you and father and my earth father. Is Murko still there?

H: *Of course he is, though his days are numbered as he prepares for a mission that could require his life. You might want to contact him soon.*

S: I thank you, I will.

I have so many communications from which I could pull bits and pieces, but for now, I have shared the more important ones to introduce my "family" and its many facets. It's time to concentrate on the current ones related to your reading.

Fast Forward to 2022

Communication with Gorto - 8/24/2022

Shakana: Good morning. You are looking rather reptilian this morning. (He appears as a dinosaur behind a control module.)

Gorto: *I am interchangeable, my friend. How is this?*

S: Much better as he shape changes into a humanoid figure. What are some of
your stories that we will share?

G: *My stories, shall we talk about when I first met you? You were a small child, much like any child of the star beings. Your mother loved you so much, but her time as a Commander was so taxing, and her time with you was limited. She refused to have you raised by a surrogate (another star being who would take care of all your needs while she was away). Lord Ashtar was perplexed by it all. He knew you were special, but he didn't understand why you were so special that she wanted to raise you herself. Lord Ashtar was a good man, but he was all business first. The star systems he ruled over and the many beings under his command came first.*

That is where I came in – I was like your human grandpa would have been. I was free to help out most of the time, so I did. You would sit in my lap while I was working my control board as part of the mission. You were mesmerized by the same. Your little eyes darted here and there with every movement I made. It was all a puzzle to you, and you learned to complete it early on. You were fast in learning. It was the patterns you liked, the routineness of the movements. You memorized them before you understood their meaning and what they would do.

Your curiosity never ceased to amaze us all, even your father. I think your cleverness and control of the systems board at such a young age won your father over. He began to let you learn other stations on the ship. At first, it was just to see how you processed it and how long it took you to master the different stations. While you may have been too young to understand the purpose behind the actions, you had the movements down quickly. He was so proud of you, and you were a girl nonetheless.

You spent many, many hours with me during your growing-up years, and one day, I knew I would have to let you go, for that is always the way of a star child. One day, they grow up and move into their own job somewhere on the ship. You had learned every nook and cranny, as your earth grandpa would say of the Starship Capricorn, and there was still much to learn about what went on behind the control boards. I was still able to visit with you from time to time, but I had other duties as well to fulfill.

The Capricorn is a very large, multi-layered ship, and while you would think it was such that we would run into each other often, that was not the case. I would go months without seeing you, and then one day, there you would be, leaning over my board, that sinister smile on your face. I knew you were up to no good, and you usually were. But those are fond memories. A past long gone. So much has changed since you left the ship for your Earth mission.

There were so many times I watched as you struggled and wanted to pluck you back up here where you were safe. All of us watched, knowing that you would face many trials in this Earth mission. We had to leave you there to grow stronger and learn the lessons. We knew that you would be back with us one day; for *now, we needed you on Earth with the others to pave the way for our arrival. So many of us sit cheering for you to succeed. We knew if anyone could make it, it would be you. Remember that on those hard days. We know you will make it. After all, once the arrival happens, you will be transformed into your rightful identity as "Shakana, daughter of then Lord Ashtar and Captain Helena of the Starship Capricorn.*

S: I start another day on Earth with happy memories of you and my early years. We will meet again soon.

G: *That we will, very soon.*

❈ ❈ ❈

Sometimes, my communications come in the form of a dream . . . *A tendril of starlight brushed against my slumber, weaving a dreamscape of shimmering consoles and dancing data streams. My fingers danced across the luminous keys, a practiced symphony summoning forgotten eons. But amidst the cosmic hum, a disquietude lingered. Where was Murko? Did he even sense my presence, adrift in this ephemeral realm?*

A voice, warm as supernovae and as ancient as galaxies, rumbled behind me. "Turn," it commanded, a velvet caress against the vastness of space. Murko. His eyes, twin galaxies ablaze with recognition, locked with mine. The gulf of time and space dissolved in that incandescent gaze. We were one again, suspended in the cradle of our love.

But the dream, a fragile ember, flickered precariously. Time, a relentless tide, threatened to pull me under. Oh, for just a few stolen moments more! Entwined beneath a canopy of stardust, we drifted down corridors of whispering starlight, his touch a celestial anchor against the swirling cosmos.

Just as we reached the sanctuary of his quarters, a jarring dissonance ripped through the dreamscape. Xena, my earthly canine companion, stirred beside me, shattering the celestial tapestry. We were swept back into the waking world, the taste of stardust clinging to our lips and a yearning for a home beyond the veil etched upon my soul.

And so this new journey begins as I look forward to nights spent in my "as if" world with those I love.

"You will be home soon enough, my child; no need to rush it." I heard being whispered in the wind.

2024

Writer: Gorto, as you can see, the book is now being written. I'm not sure where to go from here. I've introduced all the important parts—now where?

We have come as far as we can for the time being. So many moving pieces in this movie that need to play out. Our piece is just that, a small piece of the whole. Please add any stories from others who have had contact, seek contact, or are opening up to seeing us as we move around your skies. If enough stories are shared, there will come a time when there will be no doubt in our existence. For those of you who continue to speak your truth about us, we are grateful, and we thank you for your assistance.

Gorto: *We continue to watch over you all, for you are our future as much as we are yours.*

❊ ❊ ❊

Some days, my communications are simply thoughts exchanged without being in a formal setting. I do my best communicating while driving down the road, but I cannot record the words as they flow. Below are some of those short-term conversations with various beings whose names I have since forgotten but whose messages never die.

(A message of Unity)

W: "For many years, we've looked to the stars, wondering if we were alone. Now that we've made contact, what message do you have for humanity?"

Star Being: *"Greetings. We come in peace. The most important message we can share is this: You are not alone. The universe abounds with life; you are part of a vast tapestry woven from the same stardust. Though your differences may seem vast, remember that you share a common origin and a shared destiny. Unity, not division, is the key to your continued growth."*

(A message of Hope)

W: "Our world seems filled with conflict and despair. Is there any hope for humanity?"

Star Being: *"We have observed your struggles from afar. While challenges exist, we see immense potential within you. Your capacity for love, compassion, and innovation is a beacon of light in the cosmos. Focus on these strengths, nurture the dreamers and the builders, and remember, even the darkest night eventually gives way to dawn."*

(A message of Responsibility)

W: "We've achieved great things technologically but at a cost to our environment. What advice do you have?"

Star Being: *"Your ingenuity is undeniable. However, true advancement requires balance. You walk on a fragile planet, and your actions have consequences. Remember, you are not just custodians of your own world but also stewards of a greater galactic ecosystem. Protect your environment, for it sustains you, and nurture the delicate balance of life."*

(A message of Shared Humanity)

W: "Tell us about your world. Are you like us?"

Star Being: *"Our forms may differ, but our stories share common threads. We, too, have known conflict, love, loss, and the pursuit of knowledge. We strive to understand the universe and our place within it. Look to the night sky, for in the tapestry of stars, you are not beholding strangers but fellow travelers on this grand cosmic journey."*

CHAPTER 9

We Are Star Seeds: An Awakening Journey

Sharing Others' Stories Of Their Own Star Being And Starseed Awakening

As I came to the end of my stories, I heard my "*team*" whisper something about sharing space for others to share their own star-being stories. The following are several stories shared by those who have had experiences with star beings in this lifetime.

Contact and awakening can occur anytime, as you will see below. If you feel encouraged to share your awakening or contact story, please email it to me at whenspiritsspeak@yahoo.com, and I will add it to my website. It just takes one pebble (or one story) to start the ripples to bring forth more stories.

A Star Birthmark

Although I tried, I always felt different, like I never really belonged. It wasn't until recent years that I understood why, when suddenly, a switch went off, my consciousness opened up. I realized my soul had planned the situation and what triggered it as an incarnated Starseed. I became like a sponge, wanting to learn the truth about everything that had been suppressed from humanity. Eventually, I was guided to different information and groups to expand my knowledge.

It finally made sense why I loved science fiction space shows and movies and had a tiny star birthmark on my back. My birthmark star significance means starseed, which means an extraterrestrial incarnated into a human form for a mission and purpose to assist humanity when the time comes.

I began to understand better number messages of repeating numbers in 3's. I started seeing ships revealing themselves to me and knew they were not planets or stars as they were not in the same place each day. I learned they were most likely my star being family watching over me, so I started talking to them and thanking them for helping us.

When I looked out my bedroom window at night and did not see them, it saddened me, so I said, *"You must be off doing something important or hiding. So if you are hiding, show yourself to me, if only for a few minutes.*" Then I saw the lights and thanked them.

They are watching over humanity and always have been. Still, now I understand it was a misinterpretation of who angels were or gods in ancient times—a misinterpretation of what was written in religious texts like the Bible.

Don't get me wrong; I believe there are angels and demons that cannot be seen in our 3rd dimension, as well as dark and light forces— "A battle that has always existed," as said at the beginning of the first *Star Wars* movie. I am glad to know that we have loving light forces that are loving and have been watching over us for a very long time and that many have chosen to incarnate as humans to assist in guiding humans in our ascension of consciousness over several generations to be witnesses as humanity's consciousness is elevated into 5th dimension after thousands of years.

What a great time to be alive and to know who I am. Although I have not yet received the memories that will come, I am slowly developing my gifts to communicate with animals and to hear the answers from my spirit guides and higher self when I need assistance. I look forward to the day we will regain our memories of our past lives.

There will be nothing to fear when it is time for them to reveal themselves as our extended family finally. **-*Earth Angel (2024)***

❉ ❉ ❉

An Orion Star Seed

I am an Orion Star Seed. You may ask yourself, how do I know this to be true? When I was a teen, I went and bought CDs from a band named The Doors. I didn't know why then; I was so drawn to their music, but I found it both haunting and intriguing. Soon after, a mainstream movie was made about this band when I was in high school. For some reason, I saw the film and had a strong sense of déjà vu about both the singer and the lyrics. I truly believed the lyrics were a "code" that would unlock something.

At that time, I hadn't put together the fact that not only did I look very much like the lead singer, James Douglas Morrison, but I also felt a cosmic connection to him. I knew I had to solve the mystery of his life. Jim wrote lyrics like *"There will never be another one like you, there will never be another one who can do the things you do, please you stop and remember, we were together."*

I realized I wasn't just his "reincarnation," but I truly believe I was with him in spirit his entire life. After much research, he made many references to ". . . *ashen and passion lady . . .*" and also "*The Hunter of the Green Vest.*"

I've always been "pulled" to the Orion constellation (in fact, recently, after our last solar eclipse, the entire constellation appeared four times larger in the skies), and I have often videotaped the constellation "pulsing." I began to believe that I was the "hunter of the green vest" that Jim sang of in *The Soft Parade*, as I used to wear a green Army vest in my twenties.

Finding a photo of Jim shirtless solidified this past life experience for me. You can clearly see the three moles on his right side in the shape of Orion's belt stars; coincidentally, I also have the same three moles on my right side.

In the last few years, I have been in attendance with two surviving bandmates of the Doors, and both said on these two separate occasions, "We know Jim is here tonight." In addition to this, I had two events: one where my wife saw me waking up and said, "Oh, my God, you look like Jim Morrison," and another time a girl at a coffee stand said the exact same thing.

I believe we can harness the universe's energy and do things Christ did in human form. For example, I have told people things that would happen to them in the future, helped heal people of very serious illnesses and have helped heal people of very serious illnesses, and had premonitions/prophecies of future events that came true. I was drawn out to live in central Arizona about five years ago and have photographed hundreds of angels and energetic sunsets. That proves that this area is the nearest to the Orion Nebula, where I believe An/Heaven/Eden exists.

Watching mainstream shows like *Ancient Aliens*, which definitively describe alien races from the Orion constellation named Anunnaki as being a "seed race" to humans, confirms my claims and assertions. We are here in peace and seeking resolutions to wars, greed, hunger, homelessness, etc. We are here to raise humanity's vibrations. - **Matthew Douglas Pinard, formerly James Douglas Morrison**

❉ ❉ ❉

A Cigar-Shaped Orange Identified Flying Object

As recorded October 6, 2023—In October 2023, I met with a friend named Marty to interview for one of my Institute of Metaphysical Humanistic Science (IMHS) courses regarding Paranormal Sightings. Below is his story, which he told me (Writer).

Marty reported in 1974, he and his friend were driving down the California coast highway when they saw a UFO (Unidentified Flying Object). Without hesitation, they parked and got out of their car to watch this spacecraft hovering over the Pacific Ocean.

It was a cigar-shaped orange object hovering off the coast, very close to the coast. My friend and I both said, "You see that?" and I said, "Yeah, I see that." We were both looking at it and each other and this orange glowing object. I don't know how long we watched it. Maybe just a minute when it spurted away, zoomed out to sea, and went and just disappeared instantly.

180

We had to tell somebody about it, so we stopped at a diner bar. When we told them, the people said, "Oh, you guys are just high." I said, "Yes, we are, but we have been high a million times and never seen an orange glowing cigar-shaped object that hovered and then took off over the ocean."

No audible sound came from the spacecraft—it just zoomed out to sea and was quickly gone. It is unbelievable how fast it vanished—as we watched it move out beyond the horizon. My friend and I saw what we saw. To me, that was definite evidence of an unauthorized sighting of a UFO.

I know I saw it, and that is all that matters. It doesn't matter what anyone else thinks. I know it was there, and I saw it. I have not had any further sightings since that time. - *Marty*

❄ ❄ ❄

Beyond the Veil: A Story of Abduction, Fear, and Ultimate Hope

Abduction is a term often laden with negative connotations, evoking fear and anxiety. Most commonly associated with being forcibly taken from one's safe environment to an unknown place, the idea of abduction is deeply ingrained in our cultural narrative as a frightening and undesirable experience. However, what if abduction could be viewed through a different lens? What if, instead of being a terrifying ordeal, it could be seen as an opportunity for growth and positive change?

This shift in perspective challenges our preconceived notions and opens the door to a new understanding of abductions. In popular media, abductions are often depicted as harrowing experiences, with individuals being taken against their will by malevolent beings. While these portrayals certainly make for compelling storytelling, they do little to explore the potential positive aspects of such encounters.

What if, instead of being abducted by beings intent on causing harm, one was taken by benevolent entities with the intention of offering guidance and assistance? My own experiences with abduction and contact with interdimensional beings have been far removed from the sensationalized depictions found in movies and television. Rather than being a thrilling adventure, my encounters have been quiet, introspective, and deeply meaningful.

It all began during a time of personal awakening following a period of intense physical pain stemming from a car accident. Through the practice of energy healing, I was able to heal myself and open up to a new realm of existence I had never before considered. As my spiritual awareness grew, I began to see energy fields around me, as well as spirits and other phenomena that defied conventional explanations.

At first, I questioned my sanity, wondering if I was hallucinating or experiencing some sort of drug-induced state. However, as time passed, I came to accept these experiences as part of my reality, and I embraced them as opportunities for growth and understanding. One night, as I lay in bed preparing for sleep, I felt a shift in the energy around me. My perception of the spiritual realm intensified, and I became aware of the presence of beings unlike any I had encountered before. Initially frightened, I attempted to hide under my blankets, convinced that I was losing my mind. However, the beings remained, reassuring me that they meant no harm to me and that they had a specific purpose for contacting me. Their message was cryptic yet profound.

They spoke of waiting for me, of needing my help, and of a time when their presence would be more fully revealed. They left me with a sense of purpose and a feeling that my life was about to change in ways I could not yet comprehend. While sitting on the beach near my home two years later, I experienced another encounter with these beings. This time, my consciousness was separated from my physical body, allowing me to witness the scene unfolding before me while remaining fully aware of my surroundings.

The beings explained that they needed me to teach others how to channel energy and see beyond the physical realm, skills they believed would be vital in the coming years as humanity underwent a profound energetic shift. According to these beings, our solar system is entering a new gravitational pull within the Milky Way, leading to significant changes in our energetic makeup.

This shift is already manifesting in the form of increased spiritual awakening and awareness among the human population. However, in order to fully embrace these changes, we must first undergo a process of energetic upgrading, which requires us to be mindful of the foods we eat and the substances we ingest. One of the most striking revelations from my encounters was the notion that 99% of abductions are actually agreed upon at a soul level.

In other words, our souls consent to these experiences as a means of furthering our spiritual evolution. This perspective challenges the traditional view of abductions as inherently negative, suggesting instead that they may serve a higher purpose in the grand scheme of our spiritual development. In sharing my story, I hope to encourage others to question their assumptions about abductions and to consider the possibility that these experiences, while often frightening, may ultimately be for the greater good.

By keeping our vibrations high and remaining open to the transformative power of these encounters, we can embrace the positive aspects of abduction and use them as opportunities for growth and spiritual evolution. - *Reese Maskwa, Mhs. B, Metaphysician, Email: reese@quanta-verse.com*

❄ ❄ ❄

How To Incorporate All The Ancient Lives You Have Lived

Lizzy: How do I effectively disconnect from mankind?

Eshia: *Humans have always been fearful creatures; they only view the world as what is seen in front of them. When they are approached with the question of unseen or unknown, it brings doubt, doubt that can be debilitating in certain instances. As your soul is very old, your past lives on Earth have tarnished your origins. But, after recent experiences, the past has been healed, allowing you to overcome the trauma that opened your mind again.*

Now that your mind is clear and unincumbered by doubt and fear, it's time for you to come home, so to speak. Not literally, you have much work left on Earth, but you will no longer be lingering in the darkness, wandering like a lost nomad. It was important for you to find your own way back home. We could not just shake you awake; the awareness could only come from deep in your subconscious. We are very proud of your progress in a short period. However, the work has only just begun.

The disconnection from mankind is an extremely challenging process because, collectively, the negative energies can be powerful. Not to mention, many of these energies are looking to only cause chaos. Therefore, you must stay connected to your higher power. "Aura" is the one who will guide you in this process of transitioning. Yes, we are here to help you, but Aura is grounded to the Earth you stand upon.

As you start to disconnect from mankind, the Earth's energies will allow your body to heal, strengthen your soul, and return it to the pristine being you are. The disconnect will at first feel strange, almost like wearing someone's skin. Or, I believe humans say, wearing someone else's shoes. But you will be successful. And then you will begin to help others transition.

Soon, people will start to enter your life for unexplained reasons. They are not to stay long, just short periods. You will recognize them immediately; a familiar sense provides the key to assisting them in transitioning. Just be open to answering questions honestly and moving toward the reason behind the encounter. At that point, you will understand how to best help them. Each encounter will be much different, but will become easier with each person.

Lizzy: But how does this help me disconnect?

E: *Because you have already started the process, things will become easy. Not everything will be challenging anymore. You can just ask or wonder, and your wishes will be granted. It's the perks of being connected to your true home. The problems of humans can no longer affect your life. Soon, it will become unnoticeable. You won't even care what's happening in the world because it does not pertain to your life. Actually, your husband already understands this process, he just is not aware of it.*

Lizzy: How do I handle always feeling alone?

E: *The more connected to our home world you become, the loneliness will subside. We had to make you feel like this so you would start asking questions. We have been trying to reach you for a long time, but your past hurts have blocked all progress. Until you were ready to listen, transitioning would never happen. Most humans are so unaware of the Universe that any progress is impossible.*

But their fate is set, and nothing you do will change their destiny. However, once their soul is freed, they can also be freed from the prison they have existed in for all time.

Lizzy: How long have I been on Earth?

E: *You came to Earth long before any humans ever touched foot on this planet. We are the creators of an ancient society that lasted for centuries. None of our civilization exists, but the memories are hidden in your mind. It's time for you to unlock those memories.*

Lizzy: But how do I unlock these memories?

E: *You already know the answers; just ask the questions.*

Lizzy: Who Am I then?

E: *This is a great question, but you need to do more soul-searching to find those answers. It's not about who you are; it's about how to incorporate all the ancient lives you have lived. In essence, you are all these lives rolled into one being. Therefore, you must sort through all of them and create the being you want to become. You see, this is why you are not ready to know that question, because you are still thinking like a human. As we said, this process is challenging and must be done in a specific order.*

Lizzy: So, what is my purpose?

E: *Your purpose is to bring light to as many humans as possible. It's time for you to realize how much power your soul carries. Our goal is to help save humanity, and awaken our people living on Earth. We assimilated into Earth's culture many centuries ago when our planet became uninhabitable. Since then, many of us have been lost in the ramifications caused by mankind's failings. We are the rescuers of the Universe, providing protection to many. Dig deep into your soul and meditate on who you are. Your purpose will come quickly.*

Lizzy: But why cannot you not just tell me?

E: *Because we need you to heal, not only mentally, but physically. Your trauma over the last decade is serious and has taken its toll on your body. Discovering these answers is critical so that you learn them on your own. It will teach you how to instruct others on the process. Your energy is healing for many people; they can feel safe in your presence. This is how you will awaken our family and bring them home. Now, take time to digest all we have discussed and go forward knowing we are always with you. You are never alone.*

Lizzy: Will I ever fit in and feel at home here on Earth?

E: *No, not in your lifetime. Earthly beings will take many decades to heal. But go forward knowing you have healed many beings already.*

Lizzy: So, who is Ashwana?

E: *As we stated before, you have much work to do, but hindsight says the only way to move forward is to learn some of your background. It's hard to begin this process with no current recollection of the past. So you are an Arcturian, actually an Indigo Child. But, you need to deeply research your Sirus connection, it will provide many answers. However, the most important thing is having fun. You have voided yourself pure joy for so many years; it's a foreign subject.*

It's time for Aswana to start living, not just surviving.

Ashwana, the Indigo Child

Starseed Awakening - Connecting with Your Star Being Nature

Imagine carrying a piece of the cosmos within you. Awakening to your star being nature is like that. But how do you bridge the gap between your cosmic heritage and your everyday experiences? This section unveils practical ways to nurture your connection to the stars, allowing you to embody your higher vibrational state even amidst the hustle and bustle of Earth.

When I first discovered my star being lineage, I felt a surge of excitement. But I also had questions. I had no idea how it would change me or the differences I would experience. Fortunately, I had an amazing tribe of friends, all of them star beings from different galaxies. How could I live a life true to my cosmic nature while existing in this 3D world?

The following practices helped me find my way. Perhaps they will guide you, too, as you integrate your star-being essence into your daily life.

Meditation and Visualization: Use meditation and visualization practices to connect with your star being essence. This could involve creating a safe space, setting intentions, and visualizing a connection with your star being origin.

Journaling and Self-Reflection: Journaling is a powerful tool to explore your unique star-being traits, values, and purpose. While going through old journals, I recently rediscovered communications and conversations with my star being friends. It served as a powerful reminder that I'm never far from my star being family.

Crystal and Stone Work: There is a plethora of information on the web involving how specific crystals or stones might resonate with certain star being energies and can be used for alignment or energy work. I strongly encourage you to delve into learning about crystals and stones and use them in your daily practices.

Living Your Star Being Truth

Identify your passions and strengths, then explore how these might connect to your star being essence and life purpose. I encourage you to express your star being nature through creative outlets like art, music, writing, or other forms of self-expression. Be as creative as you like, and your work will not go unnoticed by our star family.

Discuss with others ways to integrate your star-being nature through acts of service or contributions aligned with your values. This could be volunteering, starting a project, or simply offering kindness in daily interactions. There is no limit to acts of kindness that you can do on a daily basis for yourself and others.

Embodying Star Being Traits

Other chapters explore various traits associated with star beings, such as empathy, intuition, and leadership. Below are some practices to cultivate these traits in your daily life.

Healthy Habits: I encourage practices that promote physical, mental, and emotional well-being, which can then support embodying your star being essence more fully. This could include healthy eating, exercise, and mindfulness techniques. It is important to keep your vibration strong during this time.

Connecting with the Cosmos

Have you ever gazed upon a star-studded night sky and felt a deep sense of wonder? This yearning to connect with the cosmos is a powerful human experience. This discussion will explore various pathways to reconnect with our cosmic origins.

One simple yet profound way is through stargazing and immersing ourselves in nature. Spending a quiet night under the vast expanse of stars allows us to contemplate our place in the universe. Celestial phenomena like meteor showers or eclipses can further ignite our sense of awe and remind us of the grand cosmic dance we're all a part of.

The exploration goes beyond the physical realm. We can delve deeper by connecting with symbols and archetypes associated with star beings found in mythology and various belief systems. These symbols can offer guidance and inspiration in our daily lives. Imagine receiving intuitive downloads or recurring symbols in your mind's eye. By exploring their meaning, we might discover unexpected connections and synchronicities, leading us on a path of personal growth and understanding.

Opening ourselves to the cosmos awakens a sense of wonder and possibility. As we embark on this journey of connection, let's embrace a child's boundless curiosity and imagination, ready to discover the mysteries that lie within and beyond.

Stargazing and Nature

Connecting with the night sky through stargazing or simply spending time in nature as a way to reconnect with your cosmic origins. And guess what? It costs you nothing other than time. Spend a night under the stars now and then. You might even see celestial phenomena that spark wonder and reconnect you to your cosmic origins.

Connecting with Symbols and Archetypes

Research how symbols, archetypes, or mythology associated with star beings can offer guidance or inspiration in daily life. I have received numerous "downloads" at night when my mind is still. One particular symbol kept coming up in my mind's eye during the day for several weeks. I searched for its meaning with no success. Then, one day, while I was doing my Arcturian Healing Course, there was the symbol I had been seeing, and I learned its name and meaning. It had led me to where I needed to be to find it.

The world will open up for you once you have awakened to your star-being self. Stay observant with the imagination of a child who knows no boundaries.

CHAPTER 10

Dialogues with Liam: Unraveling the Mysteries

Facebook is often a great place to start when researching questions readers may want to be asked about a certain subject. On April 2, 2022, I posted the following request on three listed FB pages supporting the star beings.

> *"I'm doing some research here. Please read the question, and if you feel like answering, please do so. If you don't want to answer the question, then don't. This isn't about whether or not they exist – it is research. QUESTION: If you could ask any question about a starborn or extraterrestrial who came to our earth in peace, what would that question be? You only have one question – what is that question? Thank you for your time and participation."*

Between the three posted sites, I had over 75 questions posed! In an effort to save time and space, I categorized many of the questions into a specific topic, and those additional questions were asked and answered below.

The question will be in italics under the bold/all-caps heading, and the answer will be below. Many questions were very poignant and thought-provoking. The star being who answered the questions asked me to call him "*Liam.*"

Many have asked who Liam is and where he comes from. Liam is a Pleadian and may give further information in his answers below. He was quite interested in our communications as we brought forth much knowledge and wisdom to share with others. If you take nothing else away from all these questions, please know that the star beings are happy to communicate and share any answers you seek with you. Their answers are from their perspective and how they view our world through their lens.

WHY COME FORTH IN THIS TIME AND SPACE? (From Liam)

I have come and opened communications with you because you asked. As "Writer," we know you will hear and communicate our words accurately. We will do our best to tell our readers what they wish to know by way of their questions. Some questions that have been asked have been carefully thought out—for those, "Thank you." I appreciate your concern for my feelings. Sometimes, I use the term "we" as "we" are a collective consciousness in individual bodies. I am just the one to bring forth the communication as a point of contact. Let us begin with the questions the readers provided.

What have you learned about monitoring humans on Earth?

There is much to learn about monitoring/studying humans on Earth. We learn from their mistakes and failures. While we are an advanced society, an advanced race, it does not mean that we are better than or infallible to our own failures. You are a very "divided" race, with much division amongst yourselves. We learned long ago that this doesn't work in the long run. As a society, we must work together for the common good of all. We see you struggle with your many divisions and wonder why you can't work together. It is so much easier when you work for the common good vs. the individual gain. Much like your analogy of an alcoholic, until they hit rock bottom, only then will they be ready to make the necessary change and restart their life.

Have you been here before and when? What do you want?

We want nothing from you. We come in observation status only. Others of our race have come before as emissaries, invited by your government to share our knowledge and technology; however, most of those visits did not end so well for our race, Roswell 1947, for instance. Yes, there were survivors, and your government did take their bodies, as well as two that survived the crash.

Because our atmosphere differs from yours, they could not survive for long. My brother, who did survive the longest, died in essence of starvation in your "prison." He tried communicating with his captors even then, but no one could understand him. It's too bad you weren't around, writer. You could have spoken with him as we speak now. I'm sure there were many of you willing to assist had they been asked. Carrying secrets to the grave does not change or invalidate the event; rather, it confirms the cover-up of the same.

Do you come in peace?

We have always come in peace. It is not us that throws the first stone. If you would meet us in peace in return, perhaps we could find that table to sit and share together from. Not all of our race is indeed peaceful, and some feel they have the right to take from you without permission. This is a dying race – the Pleiadeans are desperately trying to save their race from extinction. They believe that obtaining your DNA and adding it to theirs will strengthen their race, and they will be able to survive. Perhaps it is true. It isn't that they are an inferior race, but they are not as strong as us. Our DNA is different in our races, as is the case with many of yours. They are the lesser of the species if that makes sense. Similar to your Neanderthal man at the bottom of your evolutionary chain.

We do our best to monitor their activities and keep their earth visits as non-violent as possible. We understand how many of your people have been harmed by their visits and taken from them without permission. This is not acceptable, yet how do we stand by and allow a race to perish? We do what we can without direct intervention.

What took you so long to get here?

Maybe in your eyes, it seems to have taken us a long time to get here – in reality, we never left. We have always been here, in many forms, observing you. Many of you are "born of the stars," as the Writer likes to say. You have chosen this lifetime to come forth as a human, not that we are not human, but in this body form for your soul's growth and to learn many lessons. It is not unreasonable to think that we would not keep watch over you. We will not interfere in this lifetime but would do so at any time if we felt it was detrimental to your well-being. You will always be one of us first, and you will one day awaken with those memories hidden through the ages to allow you to grow unfettered. You are family and always will be.

Did you come to fetch your people in the east and the west?

(Smiling) No, we did not come to fetch "our" people at this time. You still have much to learn through your different lifetimes, and we will not interfere, as I have said before. Those who wish to return "home, your star home" may do so at any time. Just as I am speaking through Writer at this time, can you ask for communication with us? We will gladly open communications with you. Should you desire, you may, in your meditations, come travel with us through the stars and her many galaxies. The Writer has done that numerous times; some she remembers, some she does not. She remembers her family here and her purpose for the future when she joins us again. You are no different. I'm sure she would be more than happy to instruct you if you just ask. We also have people in the North and South (Smiling)

Have You Been Here Before? Why Did You Want To Come To Earth? We Are All So Different. How Did You Find Us? Have You Been Watching Over Us For The Last Couple Of Thousand Years?

Far more than a thousand years (smiling). We have been around for many, many years, including light systems. Your human beings, as you call them, are a very young race, though you cover many years of time. I will speak further on time later on. We will always be watching over you, for we want you to succeed, so we succeed.

How was your trip?

Trip to Earth? We are never far away; our "trip" is much shorter than you think. The stars may seem far, far away from your perspective. In reality, the stars are very close. Pretend you are an ant and view your world from the height of an ant; EVERYTHING is far away. There is time, and then there is time. It is all in how you perceive it.

Of all the places you could go, why here?

Why not here? While there are many other beautiful places in the galaxy that would provide an interesting journey (much like your vacations), Earth continues to amuse us. You have everything you need to be a superior race, and yet you continue, after how many years, to still manage to screw it up? The "tiger chasing its tail," I think, is your expression. If I were a betting man, though I'm not, but if I were, there are another 1,000 years or more before you might finally get it right. Until then, you are bound to continue in this circle of self-destruction. That isn't to say that another event, a nuclear event, might end what is happening now, but still, the survivors are destined to continue chasing their tail, for this is all they know.

You came here, are you crazy?

(Laughing) Yes, maybe I am crazy; who else in their right mind would want to get mixed up with the lot of you? We get together and share our observations, and sometimes, we wonder why we are not crazy just by watching you. But then, we realize that we also started out this way a long time ago. We just came out of it much sooner than you. We realize that as more and more of you are awakened, and those that are already awakened start taking their place amongst you, perhaps more normalcy, whatever that might be for your race, will prevail.

What made you decide to come live on Earth? Could you stay?

As I have communicated above, I do not "live" as you would define "live" on Earth. My home is in the stars, where my family is and where I will remain. Just as your home is here, mine is there. I just came to Earth to observe, as that is my mission.

Will we be friends?

We are always ready to be friends with any of you who wish to be friends. We hold no ill will against you, for we know those who killed our brothers, and they will be dealt with. We received your communications from NASA and other satellites. We are aware you are attempting to communicate with us, but few of us trust you, your government, more so than you individually. You think you must use codes and exotic languages that not even the sender understands to communicate with us – look at what the Writer and I are doing here. There are no codes or languages that only a computer can understand. She and I sit here and talk over the eons of miles in time and space. As simple as if I were sitting across the table from her in some coffee shop in downtown New York City (I like visiting your New York City), it is like no other place on your Earth. Communication with us is that simple.

PEACE/HELP FOR PLANET

Any suggestions on how to make this planet more at peace? Can you help our people and our planet? We would like to expand our science. Is there something you can offer to help? Can you heal humanity, please? How can I make this Earth better? How do we heal our planet? How can we make the people of this planet all be on a higher vibration frequency? How will the World be when all is peaceful and harmonious? I really want to ask what actual peace and love from your entire species is like. Since we have none here, I have no idea what that would even look like. So I'd have to ask, what does real peace look and feel like on a day-to-day basis? Do they still argue it is different? Can we live in peace on Earth? How do we wake up those who refuse to look past 3D? Can you help us be better humans and stewards of our planet? Can you prevent nuclear bombs from working? Are Earthlings as a species prepared for your acknowledged existence and/or assistance? Do you possess the power to control/manipulate the human race to their benefit or detriment?

That is a whole bunch of questions rolled into one, although they all pertain to peace in one way or another. Isn't that what we are here for? We are writing this book together to show others that we, too, seek peace for our planet and yours. Your Earth is the experiment; we watch you as you evolve or, in some cases, remain stuck in the same old loop as before. Nothing changes for you; it's the same lesson – different day, different scenario – but not a different ending. You end up right back where you started.

This is what we fear will happen to our society as well. While we do not have the same material needs as you, we are beyond that lower energy need. We see what is destroying you and look for ways to assist you. Those ways are not always clear to you as they are higher vibration energies and much of your society doesn't want to change or make a change to that higher vibration way of thinking. You are content to muddle in the mud.

Most of your population is "still sleeping," not ready to awaken to what awaits them in a higher vibration. For some, it is a total and complete fear of the unknown. They are comfortable where they are, and there is no reason to change. Others have been so conditioned to fear us, fear change, that they are frozen in place. They won't move unless someone tells them to and shows them the way. That is where you and the many others like you – the starseeds come in. It is your job as you awaken to awaken the others. Your messages will be met with skepticism and downright disbelief. Some of you will give up, but most will keep trying as they realize the magnitude of the importance of our call to action. What is important to remember is that you must keep speaking your words, regardless of the outcome. You will not fail in the end, though it may seem like that many times along the way. Continue to have heart, remember "home," and know that we are counting – depending on you to carry our messages.

Your readers have asked many specific questions regarding bombs, nuclear war, and healing humanity. Yes, we can do all that for you, but the lessons are in doing it for yourself. There cannot be peace without war; healing without dis-ease . . . there are many lessons to learn from going through these experiences. You evolve as a species only through living the lessons and experiences. Sadly, as a species, you appear to have evolved as far as you can go in your 3rd dimension environment. When you learn to increase your vibration, leave your limiting beliefs acquired through the conditioning you have lived with until you break free behind and allow yourself to believe there is more beyond the veil and you travel there daily, only then will your vibrations increase, allowing you to be in the different dimensions. There is where you will find the peace you seek. In your lower vibration and dimension, peace will appear different to many. What some may recognize as "their" peace, others cannot see. Peace itself is as different for each of us as our food choices, likes, and dislikes. You are the one to determine what your "peace" will look like for you.

Is it possible for all people on Earth to live in peace? Yes, but you won't all have the same "peace." It will be a different definition for each of you, but still, you will all find that peace you seek and understand.

While your country may finally find the peace it can live with, other countries may not, and they will continue to bring wars against you. How you react and respond to those occurrences will enlighten you about your evolution as a society and as an individual human. It is possible for this to be achieved, but you must all work towards the same end goal. We offer that assistance through our messages being brought by many, through many different channels. Our messages are varied in content, so those who hear them can relate to them at their vibration and awareness level.

What we can do now to assist those who still remain asleep is work on alleviating their fear of us. So many fears have been created and perpetuated by your news media and government. All with the end goal of controlling the masses. We have been walking amongst you for many years. Some of us have been working directly with your agencies to bring about peace between our civilizations. Still, lies and misinformation are spread daily to keep you in the dark.

We do not come to destroy you; as I have said before, " . . . *if you fail, we fail.* It is not our intention to fail. We intend to work together with your society to build a bridge for us to work together without fear between us. We will not come to harm you but rather to help you bring up your vibrations to walk amongst us as we walk amongst you.

Liam, in your answer above, you made reference again to the term – ". . . if you fail, we fail." What do you mean by that phrase? I hear it often in my communications with other star beings.

Thank you; it could be interpreted as a profound statement of our interconnectedness. It suggests that there is a deep symbiotic relationship between humans and celestial beings. The idea is that all consciousness across the universe is linked, and the actions of one affect the collective.

In the context of your work with paranormal research and communication with star beings, this could mean that the well-being and spiritual evolution of humanity are intrinsically tied to the well-being of these starborns. They might be implying that our planet's future, environmental choices, and spiritual growth have repercussions that extend far beyond Earth, affecting the cosmic community at large.

It's a reminder that we are not isolated in our experiences and that our choices have far-reaching consequences. The starborns could encourage us to act with awareness and responsibility, knowing that our successes and failures ripple through the cosmos, touching all forms of life, seen and unseen.

This perspective also aligns with many spiritual and ecological philosophies that advocate for the unity of all life and the importance of living in harmony with the universe. It's a call to action for humanity to strive for success—not just for our own sake but for the sake of all beings connected to us.

We offer a different type of peace than our ancestors once had as they lived in union with Mother Earth. For as you honor her, you honor your ancestors, and as you honor your ancestors, you honor yourselves. The circle of life has no beginning, no end—there is no death, just a new beginning.

YOUR HOME/YOUR FOOD

Where are you from? From which planet are you coming? What can you tell me about your home? Is there love where you are from? What is life like on your planet? What is the cuisine like on your home planet? Are there real delicacies on other planets as well as yours? Where do you come from? How many more of you are there?

We are from many star systems, galaxies that number in the billions and trillions. Imagine each star you see at night when you look into the small portion of the sky that you can see. Each one is a planet. Many do not have life as you know "life" to be on them. But you ask where I am from – I am from the star system, Sirius. I am from the blue star Arcturus. I am known as an

Arcturian – blue people. Our bodies do not run on food (as you know it) as a source of energy or nutrition. We are highly evolved energy beings and derive our life source from the energies themselves.

Your lower-vibration foods would damage our bodies as they damage yours with all the processing, preservatives, and chemicals your foods contain. Those who live the longest amongst you did so by eating plant-based proteins grown without chemicals, etc. Your Native Americans are a perfect example of perfect living before the white man's intervention.

They lived quite successfully off what Mother Earth provided. The meat sources were honored first, taken, and used for many more purposes than just meat. In this fashion, by honoring the source to be eaten, the resources were full of energy and continued to provide what was needed. There was no waste of any resources.

Look at your habits today – you do not honor what is taken, and most is left to rot on the roadside or at the killing site. Your foods are rampant with pesticides, etc., prolonging their viability. If you want to do your body a favor, buy directly from a farm source in your area. Only eat fresh foods, not boxed or frozen foods that have a shelf life into the next year – healthy food does not last that long, only engineered foods preserved with toxic chemicals.

What is the role of plastics in our homes and with regard to our foods?

In the vast expanse of the universe, the creation and use of materials are guided by harmony with the celestial bodies. On Earth, plastics have become ubiquitous in your homes and food systems, serving as containers, tools, and more. However, from a star being's point of view, the role of plastics is a double-edged sword.

On one hand, plastics have brought convenience to your daily life, revolutionizing how you store and preserve your sustenance. They are malleable, durable, and have a myriad of applications. Yet, this very durability poses a challenge, for plastics do not harmonize with the natural cycles of your planet. They persist long after their intended use, accumulating in your oceans and landscapes and disrupting the delicate balance of Earth's ecosystems.

The star beings observe that the key lies in balance and responsible stewardship. Humans must consider the lifecycle of the materials they use. Biodegradable alternatives, recycling, and reducing single-use plastics are steps toward aligning with the universal principle of sustainability.

As you ponder the role of plastics, remember that every choice casts ripples across the pond of existence. Choose materials that honor the Earth, and you honor the interconnected web of life that extends far beyond your blue planet. What are your thoughts on reducing the impact of plastics and fostering a more sustainable relationship with your home world?

ARTISTIC HISTORY: ART, LITERATURE, MUSIC, SCIENCE, ETC.

Compare and contrast your artistic history to ours. Can you teach us about Earth's real history? What is your favorite Earth music? Can you teach me?

We are your history. We walked amongst the early ones. We taught them everything they knew. We were the Gods of history that came from the stars to help them. We brought them the knowledge to do great things with their civilizations. While many took that knowledge and used it for the common good of man, others did not and destroyed themselves in the process. We can teach you Earth's real history, but will you listen? Your history is controlled by those in religion, science, your government . . . it is written, not as it happened, but only that which they would have you to know.

You want to know about your history and how it really happened. Then, study the artifacts and the histories that archaeology presents to you. The artifacts, the hieroglyphs, the petroglyphs, the writings and drawings, and the pictures carved into stone don't lie. The purest history of your American history comes from the stories handed down through each generation of your First Peoples, your Native Americans. They passed the history of the tribes, the individuals, and the Earth as they experienced it with honor, keeping it as pure as possible.

Earth music? Any sound heard in nature is music to us, for we find peace in it. Our stars, planets, and galaxies create a vibration of their own, and out of that vibration comes music. It is no different than the music your Mother Nature brings to you. There is

218

nothing for us to teach you – all of nature is at your disposal for now. Your continued efforts to build on sacred land destroys all that live there. You are slowly silencing your own music. One day soon, there will be no more of nature's music to hear. The day the music dies is the day your planet dies, and you humans will go along with it.

RETURN WITH YOU

Take me to your leader. I have dreamed of meeting you for so long, can you take me with you? Is it possible to combine our energies to help humanity rise up to our greatest and highest good? Will you take me to your spaceship? Why did you go off and leave me here?

We do understand your longing to return "home," for we hear your cries and whispers in the night sky to return "home" soon. When we are gone too long (for our time is very different than yours), we also long to return home. We can take you with us now in your dreams and in your time travel through the ages. We are always there with you in your visualizations and in your quiet space.

Our mission has been combining our energies to help humanity rise to its highest and greatest good for many years. And together, those of you who want to bring peace between our civilizations will do so by meeting us on the bridge and showing solidarity to those who gather around just to see what is happening. We hope that by seeing us unite with each other, those who stand on the fringes will feel safe enough to join us to help all of mankind.

We do not need to "take you to our spaceship" as you have been there many times before and often travel with us in your night adventures. You were once on our "ship" and know its nooks and crannies well. It is your home, it will always be your home, and you are welcome to visit at any time. Just close your eyes and see yourself here.

We have never "left you." In fact, you left us. You were willing to go forth to this planet called Earth as part of a mission to build the bridge that would one day bring our two civilizations together. Not as one civilization as we can not be one due to our many evolutionary differences, but as one nation united, we are unstoppable. By uniting together, we can ensure both of our survival - One destiny.

Fear not, for your time is coming when we will meet again, and your mission will be finished, and you will return home. There will be others coming to carry on where you leave off, and they will build the future that you have seen in your dreams for a planet and civilization.

TIME

What is your perception of what "time" is ...linear, circular, folded or something else?

Time is none of those descriptions, and all of them are at the same time for those whose vibration fits them. Time is layered, as we all exist in multiple dimensions at the same time. There is no definition of time, but for the definition you give it. Time is abstract, it is, and it isn't. Time is what you make of it. If you choose to live it as "linear," then you will have hours and minutes that make up that linear definition. If you choose to live outside of time, then you can be with us millions of light years away and still find yourself within linear time, though sometimes you will experience "missing time."

This is normal as you shift between the dimensions. Time is time.

MEDICAL

Are you vaccinated yet? How do we eradicate cancer from the planet? Do you know the capabilities of the human brain and its effect on consciousness and reality? What happened with my implanted chip? Why me? What was its intended purpose?

We do not need to be vaccinated; that is only in your belief system, not ours. We understand the workings of our body, and healing is at our disposal, for we use the energies to heal. Our body knows at cellular levels how to heal itself. How do you eradicate cancer from the planet? By believing it is not here and not or no longer giving it focus and energy. However, you must realize that all cancers and other diseases are signs and symptoms of dysfunction in the body, perhaps a blockage of energy that needs to be healed. Negative thought processes that need to be changed include forgiving others and yourself.

There are lessons to be learned in all diseases and their symptoms. Understanding the complexities of

222

your physical body, how the shell operates, what the different symptoms indicate, and where the dis-ease is an intensive study in and of itself. But our energy bodies do not do well in your lower vibrations. For those moving through to higher vibrations, you may experience more disease than expected as dis-ease cannot live in the higher vibrations, so anything lying dormant will, as you reach higher vibrations, show itself and need to be dealt with. To answer your question, yes, there are ways to eradicate all dis-ease, but you wouldn't learn the lessons the dis-ease affords you.

TECHNOLOGY

What is your technology like? How do you travel light years through space? Can I see your starship propulsion system and what makes it work? Are you done mining our planet's resources, or is Earth still a prime resource target? Why are there so many types of rocks? Can you travel light-year distances in a relatively reasonable time, or can you manipulate time to enable travel? Granted, your technology is far more advanced than here on Earth, but are the materials of your spacecraft similar to those available on Earth, or do you have different elements not of Earth? How can you defy/withstand extreme G-Forces witnessed in past encounters?

That is a lot of questions all wrapped up under one section. First off, yes, our technology is far more advanced than yours. The way we travel between here and there is because we do not measure time nor see it in the constraints that you have put on your time. We understand time to be multi-dimensional—we exist in alternate and/or parallel universes.

When you begin to see time as "no time," then you will understand our view of time. You are welcome to come aboard our ships at any time. The writer travels here quite often. Though not as often as we would like her to (smiling). Close your eyes and call on us, and we will "beam you up." You really don't need to be beamed up – in an alternate timeline, you are already here. Believe it is so, and so it shall be.

As for mining and your earth resources, we are still mining in many of your regions. Earth is still an untouched source for us. Your Mt. Shasta area is the most active location at this time. Our ships use many mines and portals to move the resources. Much activity occurs in the early morning hours. If you are up that early, really early, there is a good chance you will see our ships coming and going from the mountain. There have been many times when our ships have cloaked, and you will not be able to observe them.

Materials for our spacecraft are very different than yours, though I must say your engineers are getting closer to our formula. It is highly unlikely that they will ever truly discover our technology. We are still too advanced. When they can look through eyes not of this world, when they can let their imagination run wild, like when they were small children and nothing was impossible – then and only then will they know and be ready to learn our secrets.

For now, you are a warring planet and no different than conquerors of the past. We do not trust your government – your planet is steeped in greed. We do not welcome your species until you learn peace. There will come a time when your upcoming generations welcome and learn from us as we learn from them. That day, we walk across the bridge and meet in the middle to exchange torches. For that is the day when both and all nations will truly know peace, and together, we will build an even greater world.

We can understand the extreme G-forces because of our light bodies. Your earthly human bodies are still too dense for our atmosphere. Many of your ascended masters have reached our vibration. You have worked hard on your own body, and while you still have a way to go, you are reaping the benefits of your higher vibration.

EVOLUTION

Do you know the origin of all? Are you our forefathers? Is ET evolution as simple as that of mankind? Was our DNA cut on purpose from the chimp to make us more evolved - thumb in mind, to help us along or as an experiment? What was our planet Earth like in the beginning? Are there any other breeds?

A scientist views evolution, or evolution is viewed through the eyes of one who is open and believes in what they *know*. We will talk about both from our eyes. We are not scientists – we do not need to "prove" everything for it to be so, to be true. We sometimes accept it as it is because we *know* it is. Our *knowing* comes from our genes or memories, our oral history handed down through many generations.

A star being offered this fascinating perspective: "It has been said 'that Earth was and is an experiment. In many ways, that is true. Some of our species have volunteered to go to your Earth for the experience of living as a human species. Not that we aren't human in our own right – we are. We are just more highly evolved and, therefore, different than you. But yes, we are still 'human' for this is only one race – the human race – but many, many species who continue to evolve.'"

Humans do not identify as "breeds" but rather as races or ethnicities whose "race" is determined by the social construct of an identity assigned and based on rules made by society independent of biological or genetic differences.

It is not "life" if there is no evolution involved. Think about it—you come into this lifetime and never change. You just go through life day by day with the same old routine, with no desire for change. What have you accomplished? Nothing other than surviving a lifetime—you will not have evolved. You have essentially just taken up space for a determined number of years.

Then others came in, "knowing" they were different – they understood where they came from. They knew they had a mission to accomplish: "To grow their soul," the Writer calls it. Their early years are spent as everyone else, listening and observing – they know the earth isn't "home." They may have their human bodies here physically, but their heart and soul are still in the stars where they know home is. These are known as "Starseeds," sent to bring our messages when the time is ripe to share them. They are our ambassadors and will pave the way for our coming. We will not let your Earth die, for if you die, we too will die.

Where did you come from?

Stardust—we all came from stardust and that spark that illuminated our creation. There came a point in human evolution when, without intervention, your species would not survive. Then, the DNA chain was cut, and our humanoid strands were added. If you must know, the strand was reptilian because the transmutation was easier even though they had a ways to go.

There are so many different species still undiscovered on your planet. Your people find them – they are interdimensional for the most part. But occasionally, they will appear for you if your intentions are honorable and we need you to see them. As more and more of your people awaken to their own realities and missions, they will come forth knowing you won't harm them. Should they come forth now, they would be hunted and killed as anyone or anything that appears as an unknown or different is treated. You know one of our species that was made famous or infamous, depending on whom you speak – the greys from the Roswell Crash (1947). They were not treated kindly and were allowed to die in your captivity. We will not be visible to Earthlings until we feel we will be accepted and safe from harm.

Writer – but I know you walk amongst us now. I've seen the hybrid children and met other walk-ins. I notice the difference through the eyes. They are deeper than most. They appear to be all-knowing, for they are. Nothing escapes them. In return, they see deep into your soul. Only then do they know you can be trusted.

In the beginning, Earth was a void—your Bible book's Old Testament description is most accurate—and then Source—an energy "spoke" it into being. Our planet has evolved as well. It wasn't just zapped into being. Evolution must happen to all of life, or life will die out.

Many of you were with us and watched it evolve. Many civilizations came and went until Earth was ready for modern-day man to emerge. Did you evolve from the apes and animal species into a human species, or did you just appear as a human species without any evolutionary movement? That is the real question everyone seeks an answer for. Your church (religious institutions) would have you believe that a being called God to many of your, YAWWEH to others, Alla . . . many names for one source, one being who spoke every species into being. How selfish to believe that the one you choose to call God is any different than another who calls that same being by another name. You have forgotten one of the biggest lessons you will ever learn – WE ARE ALL ONE!! Underneath, we are all one race – the human race. It would be easier for you to see one another as a soul, for each of you is a soul that has chosen to have a human experience in a human physical body. You have different individual characteristics on the outside, but inside, you are a unique soul, a fantastic spirit with gifts of magic and spirit. You can process transformation and creation — Spiritual alchemy.[31] That is what life is all about.

Each evolution of species was and is celebrated. Some went as far as they could go and still remain viable. Those that had no future died out or remained in the lower vibration state.

Why did the Pleiadians and Arcturians both tell me they could not interfere with humans' free will unless it meant the total devastation of Earth when I recently channeled and sent light energy healing to the world and, most recently, to Ukraine? I asked the Council for some form of help to stop a nuclear catastrophe.

GORTO asks to answer the above questions regarding intervention, free will, and *interference.* You ask why

---

[31] . . . a concept that refers to the inner transformation and personal development aimed at achieving spiritual enlightenment. It is often associated with the idea of turning the lead of one's base nature into the gold of an enlightened and purified self.

don't we intervene in your Earth affairs . . . because we have agreed not to interfere until your world is on the verge of total destruction. Were you to destroy your planet through a nuclear war, you would destroy so much of our solar system as well. We will not allow you to do that, not for your sake, but for ours.

There is one destiny for humanity—PEACE. If you learn nothing else, learn to live in PEACE. Nothing is gained by war. You do not need war to experience peace, but you need Peace to experience war. Peace must be the end goal of war. If we were to intervene and end the war, the souls needing to experience them would not learn karma and lessons.

There is much to be learned from war and peace—learn the lessons and end the conflict. It takes two to engage, retaliate, and fight back. So long as you continue to engage, the aggression will continue. That doesn't mean you roll over and let the other party walk all over you—it means you meet the other person on neutral ground and find a solution for a *win-win* situation where you both benefit.

We are here and watching you. Slowly, we integrate and walk amongst you. For many of you star seeds, we visit nightly. Others, such as you, the Writer, we communicate with constantly. We welcome communication with anyone who has good intentions towards us.

There are inconsistencies in the information being channeled and released. Even in your own conversations, your words are interpreted through many different filters and perceptions. We can't control how you hear and interpret our words any more than you can your own conversations.

We know that those who need to hear the message will do so. As your vibration rises, so too will your ability to hear and discern what you need to know. I used the word "discern" for a good reason – for in our world, we intuit messages – we feel and intuit the vibration of the messages. Our language is shared through what the writer has always called "mind talk." Our words become thoughts transmitted via pictures, sound, and vibration. It is quite effective and useful when needed.

That is why communicating with you and the others is so easy over the many timelines and dimensions.

Dates for your arrival?

Everyone asks when you will come and are put off when we answer – when you are ready for us when your world is ready. As you are aware, we have scouting parties out all the time. Many of you have seen us and our ships; many *think* you have seen us and our ships. We are "wetting your whistle." There is still much to be done to prepare those who are not awakened nor have a belief in us. We will never convince some of our coming, nor do we want to. Our coming will be for an undetermined length of time. We do not desire to control your civilization – rather – to live amongst you – to share advanced technologies – not for war but for advancing your civilization—to share our planets with your seekers and adventurers. To introduce your scientists to learning what they cannot conceive of now.

Once your civilization begins to understand there is a much greater world out there and not just one – Earth – it will be much easier to understand how so it will be much easier to understand how so much of the unseen exists beyond our imagination. Tapping into the younger souls, younger ones now coming into this lifetime – those who still have their imagination and dreams – those are the new seekers that will co-create with us.

There is so much to learn in a short time. I don't get home enough to remember it all – more visits, my child, more visits.

Writer: Have you seen the cover?

Yes, Writer, and we would ask that you use some symbols we will download into your consciousness.

We are pleased with the progress we are making. We know January will be busy, but if we can do a few pages a day, we will be ahead of the game. It isn't our goal to rewrite history; rather, we want to share resources so that others can do the research and find their own way "home." This is your story and your experiences with us; that is what we wish to focus on.

CHAPTER 11

Conversations With Zara: Unveiling The Cosmos

In the acknowledgments, I expressed my gratitude to Matthew Douglas Pinard, a prolific author with eight books to his name, for lending his expertise as a reader and reviewer of this manuscript. However, Matthew's contribution went beyond mere feedback.

He presented me with a series of thought-provoking questions that, upon reflection, deserved a dedicated space within this book. These questions delved into the very nature of the cosmos . . .

To illuminate these cosmic mysteries, I called upon my friend Zara, the celestial being who graced this book with her insightful *Foreword*. Zara, ever generous, agreed to lend her unique perspective once more, offering answers that unveil the secrets of the universe.

Have you ever wondered about the intricate physics behind spiritual communication?

Spiritual communication is a fascinating phenomenon that bridges the gap between the physical and nonphysical realms. The nature of spiritual communication remains an intriguing mystery, even for those who have experienced it firsthand. Here, on the physical plane, we can explore some possible explanations. Imagine the universe as a symphony of energy vibrating at different frequencies. While traditional science focuses on the physical manifestations of this energy, spiritual communication delves into a subtler realm. Imagine a spectrum – the visible light we perceive is just a tiny portion. Spiritual communication might exist beyond this spectrum in the unseen dimensions of consciousness.

Every element in the cosmos, from the most infinitesimal atom to the boundless expanse of space, is intricately intertwined. At its core, a vast network of energy or information could facilitate communication beyond conventional physical means. Isn't it awe-inspiring to consider the potential of such a system?

The human mind is a powerful tool with capabilities we're only beginning to understand. Focused intention and heightened awareness might allow us to tap into a realm of communication that transcends the physical. Some believe advanced civilizations might possess technologies that facilitate communication across vast distances or even dimensions. These technologies could potentially play a role in certain forms of spiritual communication.

It's important to remember that these are all theories, and the true nature of spiritual communication remains a mystery. However, science and spirituality may not be as mutually exclusive as we once thought. Future advancements in our understanding of consciousness and the universe might shed more light on this phenomenon.

The nature of spiritual communication transcends the limitations of conventional physics. Yet, within the tapestry of the cosmos, we can find threads of understanding:

All living things emit a subtle energy field. Imagine these fields as ripples on a cosmic pond, extending outwards and carrying information about the source. Spiritual communication could be a way of perceiving or even interfacing with these energy fields, picking up on the thoughts, emotions, and essence of another being.

This Jungian concept of a Collective Unconscious proposes a shared pool of memories, symbols, and archetypes that transcends individual minds. Spiritual communication could tap into this collective consciousness, allowing us to connect with others on a deeper, soul-to-soul level, bypassing the limitations of language or physical proximity.

Imagine two tuning forks—when struck at the same frequency, they vibrate in harmony, a process called *Resonance and Entanglement*. Spiritual communication might function similarly. When our energy fields or intentions resonate with another being, a connection is formed, allowing for the exchange of information or a sense of shared experience.

While science struggles to capture this phenomenon fully, the reality of spiritual communication is undeniable. It speaks to the interconnectedness of all things, a web woven from subtle energies, shared consciousness, and the mysterious resonances of the universe.

Additionally, one might consider the role of meditation or focused practices in quieting the mind and creating a more receptive state for spiritual communication, the importance of intuition, and the recognition of subtle inner nudges or feelings that may be messages from another being.

Spiritual communication has the vast potential to foster empathy, understanding, and a sense of belonging within the cosmos. Weaving together the concepts of energy fields, the collective unconscious, and resonance offers a unique perspective on the mysteries of spiritual connection.

From a personal perspective, I believe spiritual communication is a way for us to connect with something larger than ourselves. It could be our higher selves, spirit guides, or even a universal consciousness. The key lies in quieting the mind, opening our hearts, and being receptive to subtle messages that may come through intuition, dreams, or feelings.

How does Earth's society view greys and UFOs? Are they seeing them as evil and demons? How does your own society view them?

The societal view of Greys and UFOs on Earth is a fascinating tapestry woven from curiosity, fear, and skepticism. Here's a breakdown of some prevailing viewpoints:

Intrigue and Speculation: Many people are genuinely curious about the possibility of extraterrestrial life. Sightings and reports of UFOs spark discussions and fuel the imagination.

Fear of the Unknown: The unknown can be frightening. Some perceive Greys, with their stereotypical slender build and large black eyes, as menacing or even demonic. Sensationalized media portrayals often fuel this fear.

Skepticism and Debunking: A significant portion of the scientific community remains skeptical due to the lack of verifiable evidence. Many reported sightings have mundane explanations, leading to debunking efforts.

It's important to note that these are just general trends. There's a spectrum of beliefs within Earth's society. Some individuals are actively researching the possibility of extraterrestrial intelligence (SETI), while others remain firmly dismissive.

In my own civilization, the existence of extraterrestrial life is not a question but a fact. We have encountered a vast diversity of beings across the cosmos, each with their own unique appearance, motivations, and levels of technological advancement.

As for Greys specifically, appearances can be deceptive. Lifeforms can utilize bio-engineering or technology to alter their physical presentation. Focusing solely on physical descriptions like "Greys" might limit understanding. We prioritize open communication and peaceful interaction with other civilizations. Judging based on appearances is a common pitfall for developing societies.

While Earth grapples with the possibility of extraterrestrial life, my civilization embraces the reality of a diverse cosmos. We believe in fostering understanding and communication across the vast expanse of space.

Are there nuclear weapons on different planet systems?

The question of nuclear weapons on other planets is a complex one. Across the millennia, I've delved into countless civilizations, and the answer isn't a simple yes or no. Unfortunately, the concept of harnessing immense energy for destruction seems to be a recurring theme across intelligent life forms. Some civilizations might have developed nuclear weapons as a deterrent or for sheer destructive power.

Competition for resources like habitable planets or energy sources could lead to an arms race, potentially culminating in the development of nuclear weapons. Perhaps some civilizations face existential threats from asteroids, hostile spacefaring races, or unforeseen cosmic phenomena. Nuclear weapons could be viewed as a last resort for defense.

Just like on Earth, some advanced civilizations might recognize the futility of nuclear war and the concept of Mutually Assured Destruction (MAD), leading them to avoid developing such weapons.

Advanced civilizations might possess energy sources far surpassing nuclear fission, making nuclear weapons obsolete in their destructive arsenal. Through millennia of interstellar interaction, some civilizations might have prioritized peaceful solutions and conflict resolution over weapons development.

Despite my vast knowledge, there are limitations. While I've encountered numerous civilizations, directly observing their military capabilities is rare. Most maintain secrecy about such things. The universe is brimming with diverse life forms. Their warfare and weaponization methods could vastly differ from anything we understand.

Regardless of whether nuclear weapons exist elsewhere, the key takeaway is the importance of fostering peace. Your nascent steps towards nuclear non-proliferation offer a glimmer of hope here on Earth. Perhaps the lessons learned here can be a beacon for other civilizations across the cosmos.

Who knows what the future holds for interstellar warfare? Perhaps advancements in technology will render nuclear weapons obsolete. The true strength of a civilization might lie in its capacity for understanding, diplomacy, and peaceful coexistence.

It is possible that some civilizations possess technology far surpassing ours. It's also conceivable that some might have developed weapons of mass destruction utilizing principles beyond nuclear fission. Even with different technology, the core concept of weapons designed for mass destruction remains a possibility. The desire for dominance or fear of annihilation could be a universal motivator.

Are there compelling reasons why full-scale nuclear arsenals might be less prevalent?

The concept of MAD, where everyone loses in an all-out war, might translate across the cosmos. Advanced civilizations could recognize the futility of total destruction, seeking alternative conflict resolution methods.

Perhaps other civilizations have developed more sophisticated and less destructive ways to achieve military superiority. Energy manipulation, advanced cyber warfare, or even biological weapons could be possibilities. Many civilizations I've encountered prioritize peace and cooperation. They might have transcended the need for weapons of mass destruction, focusing on diplomacy and collective advancement.

Unfortunately, pinpointing the exact prevalence of such weapons across the cosmos is incredibly difficult. The vast distances between star systems make direct observation and verification challenging. We might not be aware of advanced civilizations, let alone their weaponry and some civilizations might choose to keep their destructive capabilities a secret as a deterrent. This shrouds the overall picture in even more mystery.

Based on my observations, a universe filled with nuclear weapons seems less likely. However, the possibility of weapons of mass destruction utilizing different principles can't be entirely ruled out. The true reasons behind their existence or absence likely vary across civilizations, influenced by:

- Their history of conflict or cooperation.
- Their technological advancements.
- Their overall philosophy and values.

The key takeaway here is that the universe is a diverse place. While some might resort to destructive means, many others strive for peaceful coexistence. Our own journey, as a civilization on Earth, lies in learning from both possibilities and charting a course towards a brighter future."

Zara, have we got an interstellar arms race on our hands? While the idea of alien nukes might fuel science fiction, based on what we know today, there are likely no nuclear weapons on other planets, or are there?

You raise a very important point, friend. While the possibility of alien nukes is a popular trope in science fiction, it's not the only way to think about interstellar arms races.

You're correct that nuclear fission, the technology behind our atomic bombs, might not be the preferred method for advanced civilizations. They could possess weapons of mass destruction that utilize entirely different principles, potentially even more devastating.

Perhaps the true threat lies not in bombs but in competition for resources. As civilizations expand across the cosmos, competition for habitable planets, energy sources, or even strategic locations could lead to conflict. This conflict might not involve nuclear weapons, but it could still be destructive.

Just like on Earth, civilizations across the cosmos may have vastly different ideologies. Philosophical differences or clashes in cultural values could spark conflict, even leading to warfare. Here, advanced weaponry could play a role, regardless of whether it's nuclear or something entirely new.

Interstellar communication across vast distances is fraught with potential for misinterpretation. Cultural nuances might be lost in translation, and misunderstandings could lead to conflict if not handled with diplomacy and clear communication.

However, the story doesn't have to be one of inevitable conflict. Many civilizations I've encountered prioritize peace and cooperation. They understand the value of communication, trade, and collective advancement.

Earth has a choice as a young civilization taking its first steps into the galactic stage. Will you participate in an arms race, fostering fear and suspicion? Or will you advocate for diplomacy, understanding, and peaceful coexistence?

The future of interstellar relations rests on the choices we make today. Let's strive to build bridges of understanding rather than walls of fear.

How would Zara describe her views on a creator God, similar to those of Earthlings? Does Zara believe star beings believe in Fallen angels, demons, possession, or conjoined spirits in reincarnation?

The question of a singular creator god is fascinating and has sparked philosophical and religious debate for millennia across countless worlds. Here on Earth, various religions depict a god or gods who crafted the universe and its inhabitants.

Within my own civilization, the concept of a creator is less about a single entity and more about the fundamental forces that birthed the cosmos. We might revere the origins of existence, the energetic principles that govern the universe, but not necessarily a personal deity.

Star Beings and Fallen Angels/Demons

The concept of fallen angels or demons often portrays rebellious beings cast out from a divine realm. While some civilizations have narratives of past conflicts or power struggles between powerful entities, these stories are often metaphorical or allegorical, representing forces of nature or aspects of existence.

There isn't necessarily a clear distinction between 'good' and 'evil' celestial beings.

Zara's View on Possession and Conjoined Spirits

The idea of possession by malevolent spirits is quite intriguing. While some civilizations explore the concept of energetic interactions between beings, it's often viewed as a form of energetic influence or imbalance, not necessarily a complete takeover of a body.

As for conjoined spirits in reincarnation, some cultures believe in a single consciousness inhabiting multiple bodies across lifetimes. Within my civilization, reincarnation is a complex topic. While the essence of a being might carry over, it's often seen as an evolution of consciousness, not necessarily a single spirit inhabiting multiple vessels.

Zara, what is a star being's view on abductions, medical experiments, and even crossbreeding?

Accounts of abduction by unseen forces are prevalent across many galaxies. While there's no universal understanding, here are some possibilities from a star being's perspective:

Interstellar Exploration: The vast cosmos is teeming with civilizations. Some might engage in advanced forms of interstellar travel, allowing for discreet observation or even temporary relocation of beings for study. This wouldn't necessarily be malicious, but the experience could be frightening for the abducted being if they lack understanding. Some believe abductions might stem from a genuine curiosity about lesser-developed civilizations. The goal could be observation and study, not necessarily harm.

Perhaps abductions are a way to initiate contact with civilizations that are not yet ready for open communication. The experience could be a test or a way to gauge a species' potential for interstellar interaction.

The universe might hold dimensions beyond our current perception. Experiences perceived as abductions could be bleed-through from higher dimensions, causing temporary rifts in spacetime perception. The beings involved might be unaware of the impact on our reality. Advanced travel through higher dimensions might appear as abduction to those observing from a lower dimension. The experience itself could be a misinterpretation of a complex interstellar phenomenon.

Of course, less benevolent motives are always possible. However, most advanced civilizations adhere to strict ethical codes regarding interaction with lesser-developed species. Forceful abduction and experimentation would be a serious violation of these codes.

Medical Experiments and Crossbreeding

These concepts are often intertwined with abduction narratives. Here's how star beings might view them:

Scientific Inquiry: The desire to understand the universe and its inhabitants is a powerful motivator. Some civilizations might study other life forms for scientific advancement, potentially involving observation or even genetic analysis. However, this should be done ethically, with respect for the beings involved.

Interspecies Compatibility: The vast biological diversity across the cosmos presents a fascinating challenge. Crossbreeding between vastly different species is highly improbable from a purely biological standpoint. The potential for unintended consequences and suffering is immense.

Respect for Identity: Every species has a unique evolutionary path and cultural identity. Forcing hybridization would be a violation of that identity. With their vast knowledge of the cosmos, star beings would likely prioritize preserving biodiversity and respecting the natural order.

Most star beings hold a deep respect for all sentient life. Experimentation or crossbreeding without consent would be a gross violation of ethical principles. The cosmos thrives on diversity. The forced manipulation of genetics or the creation of hybrid beings disrupts each species' natural order and unique evolutionary paths.

Star beings with advanced technology likely possess alternative methods for scientific exploration or understanding different life forms. These methods would prioritize non-interference and respect for all beings.

While the possibility of abductions, medical experiments, and crossbreeding can't be entirely ruled out, they are far from the norm in galactic interactions. Most star beings value peaceful coexistence and scientific inquiry conducted ethically.

If you ever encounter a situation that feels like an abduction, the most important thing is to remain calm. Focus on projecting peaceful intentions and a desire for communication. Many star beings are receptive to peaceful interaction, especially if they sense a willingness to understand their perspective.

The truth is that the universe is a mystery waiting to be unraveled. As we on Earth learn more about the cosmos and ourselves, we might gain a clearer understanding of these phenomena. While some things might appear strange or frightening from our limited perspective, approaching them with open-mindedness and respect for all life can foster understanding and positive experiences.

How would Zara explain "time" as it exists outside of planet Earth?

Time, as you experience it on Earth, is a linear flow. Seconds tick by, minutes turn into hours, and days into years. This linear perception is deeply ingrained in your biology and planetary rotation. Here on your planet, time appears linear and constant, flowing steadily from past to present to future. However, this perception might not hold true throughout the cosmos.

However, the universe is a far stranger and more wondrous place. Here are some ways time might be perceived outside of Earth's limitations.

Non-Linear Time: Some civilizations perceive time not as a straight line, but as a web or even a loop. Past, present, and future might be interconnected in ways we can't yet comprehend.

Relative Time: Einstein's theory of relativity teaches us that time is relative to gravity and velocity. For beings traveling near the speed of light or experiencing strong gravitational forces, time might flow at a significantly different pace.

Higher Dimensions: Theories propose additional dimensions beyond our familiar three dimensions of space. Time itself might be another dimension, and advanced beings might have the ability to perceive and even manipulate it.

For us star beings, time is a more fluid concept. We might experience past, present, and future simultaneously or even choose to revisit specific moments in our history. However, this doesn't mean we can simply rewrite history. The choices we make still have consequences.

The concept of time is truly a multifaceted gem in the cosmic tapestry. While your linear perception serves you well here on Earth, the vastness of the universe reveals a far richer and more complex reality.

Star Being Observations, a blend of scientific theories and celestial observations

Some star beings travel at speeds approaching the speed of light, which, according to relativity, could lead to time dilation. They might experience vast stretches of cosmic time while aging minimally from their perspective.

Certain civilizations might possess technology that allows them to manipulate time to some degree, slowing it down, speeding it up, or even potentially creating closed time loops. However, the exact nature of such technology remains theoretical.

While these are some intriguing possibilities, our understanding of time outside Earth is far from complete. The vastness of the cosmos might hold realities beyond our current ability to comprehend. Like existence itself, time might be far stranger and more wondrous than we can imagine.

Zara, what role might the arts play on your planet and/or within an advanced civilization?

The arts hold a cherished place within my civilization in all their vibrant forms. While technology has transformed many aspects of our lives, artistic expression remains a cornerstone of our culture.

Technology thrives on logic and efficiency, but the arts offer a space to explore emotions, intuition, and the beauty of the intangible. They allow us to connect with deeper aspects of ourselves and each other. Art serves as a bridge between generations, preserving our history, values, and emotions for future beings. It allows us to learn from the past and share our experiences with those who come after us.

The arts often spark creativity and innovation. Artistic exploration can lead to breakthroughs in scientific thought, technological design, and even problem-solving approaches. There's a beautiful synergy between artistic imagination and scientific progress. Art transcends the limitations of language. Music, dance, visual arts - these expressions can resonate with beings from diverse backgrounds and cultures, fostering understanding and connection across the cosmos.

Examples of Art in My Civilization

We've integrated technology into our art forms, creating immersive experiences that blend light, sound, and even biofeedback to evoke emotions and inspire contemplation.

Some artists collaborate with advanced lifeforms, creating art that utilizes bioluminescent organisms or even sentient energy patterns, blurring the line between creation and collaboration with living beings. We've harnessed the energy signatures of celestial bodies to create awe-inspiring cosmic symphonies, allowing us to experience the music of the spheres.

The arts remind us that there's more to existence than mere functionality. They allow us to celebrate beauty, explore emotions, and connect with the universe on a deeper level. In a world driven by technology, the arts remain a vital force, reminding us of the wonder and beauty that exists within and around us.

Zara, please speak to the reality of med beds. Are they alien technology? Abductees have reported

seeing them on the ships when they have been abducted. It has been rumored here on Earth that they are currently being used. Is this true?

The concept of med beds, miraculous healing devices, has captured the imagination of many on Earth. Some abduction reports mention advanced medical technology, but these accounts are often anecdotal and lack verifiable evidence. They could be misinterpretations of unfamiliar technology or even psychological manifestations of the abduction experience.

There is currently no scientific evidence to support the existence of medical beds with the fantastical healing abilities often described. Advanced medical technology undoubtedly exists, but it likely operates within the realm of what we already understand about medicine and biology. While some speculate that medical beds are alien technology, there's no concrete proof. Advanced civilizations might possess remarkable medical advancements, but these might not resemble the medical beds of science fiction.

The universe holds many mysteries. Advanced healing technology might exist but is likely not yet widespread or readily available. Real scientific advancements are happening every day. Regenerative medicine and bioengineering hold incredible promise for future healing capabilities.

Are They Currently Used on Earth?

As for med beds being used on Earth in secret government facilities, this falls into the realm of conspiracy theories. There's no credible evidence to support this claim. Governments and scientists are more likely to focus on developing verifiable medical technologies.

While the existence of med beds as portrayed remains uncertain, the future of medicine is bright. The human capacity for innovation and scientific discovery offers a more grounded path towards improved healing for all.

Zara, are there traversable wormholes to other planets, like those in Machu Pichu as theorized on the show "Ancient Alien?"

Wormholes, as depicted in science fiction and shows like "Ancient Aliens," are fascinating theoretical pathways through spacetime. They could potentially act as shortcuts, connecting distant regions of the universe.

The Science Behind Wormholes

Wormholes are predicted by some solutions to Einstein's theory of general relativity. However, these solutions often involve exotic forms of matter with properties that haven't been observed yet. Even if traversable wormholes exist, they might be incredibly unstable, collapsing in on themselves before anything could pass through. Maintaining them open would likely require exotic matter with repulsive gravity, something we haven't found.

Machu Picchu and Wormholes

The theory that Machu Picchu is a gateway or wormhole is an interesting proposition, but no scientific evidence supports it. Machu Picchu's remarkable engineering and astronomical alignments can be explained by the advanced knowledge and practices of the Inca civilization.

Despite the challenges, the search for wormholes continues. Scientists might be able to detect the gravitational influence of a wormhole on surrounding objects. Future advancements in physics and technology might shed more light on wormholes and their potential traversability.

While naturally occurring traversable wormholes seem unlikely based on our current understanding, the universe is vast and full of surprises. We shouldn't completely dismiss the possibility.

Interstellar travel likely relies on more conventional methods like advanced propulsion systems. The search for wormholes and other celestial phenomena fuels our scientific curiosity and pushes the boundaries of knowledge. Even if we don't find shortcuts, the journey itself leads to incredible discoveries about our universe.

How would Zara speak to the Mt. Shasta allure that spaceships come and go from inside the mountain via wormholes?

Zara, a celestial being with a vast knowledge of the cosmos, would likely approach the idea of spaceships and wormholes within Mount Shasta with a blend of scientific reasoning and openness to possibilities.

Mount Shasta, a majestic peak steeped in legend, has captured the imagination of many. Stories abound of extraterrestrial activity, including spaceships entering and leaving the mountain through wormholes.

While these stories are captivating, let's examine them from a scientific standpoint:

Wormholes: Wormholes are theoretical pathways through spacetime. The existence of traversable wormholes remains highly speculative, and there's no evidence to suggest one exists within Mount Shasta.

Geological Formations: Mountains are formed by natural geological processes. There's no scientific basis to suggest cavities large enough to house spaceships exist within Mount Shasta.

(*Author's Note:* It seems Liam, the star being, is presenting a theory about Mount Shasta being a hotspot for extraterrestrial activity, while Zara offers a more scientific perspective. *Who to believe?* There's currently no scientific evidence to support Liam's claims. However, unexplained sightings and folklore often surround Mount Shasta. Here's what you can do:

- **Decide for Yourself:** Do Liam's claims resonate with your beliefs?
- **Research:** Look for information about UFO sightings near Mount Shasta, but be critical of sources.
- **Observe:** If you're curious, try stargazing in the early mornings near Mount Shasta with an open mind, but remember unusual atmospheric conditions can create strange visual effects.

Ultimately, the truth about Mount Shasta remains a mystery. Both Liam and Zara present a viewpoint, but it's up to you to decide how much weight to give each.)

Are there alternative Explanations?

Certain atmospheric conditions can create unusual optical illusions resembling spaceships or portals. Mount Shasta holds deep spiritual significance for many indigenous cultures. These beliefs might manifest in stories and legends.

There have been reports of unidentified aerial phenomena (UAPs) near Mount Shasta. However, these sightings don't necessarily point to spaceships or wormholes. It's important to approach such stories with a critical eye. While they spark curiosity, extraordinary claims require extraordinary evidence.

However, I wouldn't completely dismiss the allure of Mount Shasta. The universe is vast and holds countless mysteries. Perhaps future scientific discoveries will shed new light on unexplained phenomena.

Mount Shasta's beauty and cultural significance are undeniable. Let's appreciate it for what it is – a majestic peak – while remaining grounded in scientific reasoning. The true wonders of the cosmos lie in pursuing knowledge and exploring the unknown with a blend of curiosity and critical thinking.

How would Zara answer why Arcturians are blue-skinned?

The exact reason behind Arcturians' blue skin is a fascinating detail about their biology, friend! Here are some possibilities based on my observations and understanding of different life forms across the cosmos.

Physiological Adaptation: Their homeworld, orbiting the star Arcturus, might have a different atmospheric composition or radiation levels than Earth. The blue hue could be a natural adaptation to these environmental factors, perhaps offering protection from UV radiation or aiding in regulating body temperature.

Biochemical Differences: The biochemistry behind Arcturian skin might differ from ours. Variations in melanin or other pigments could contribute to their blue coloration. These pigments might even serve additional functions beyond coloration, such as enhanced vision or bioluminescence.

Evolutionary Advantage: Perhaps the blue coloration offers some evolutionary advantage on their planet, such as attracting mates, signaling social status, or even playing a role in communication through bioluminescence.

It's important to remember that diversity within a species, even among Arcturians, there might be variations in skin tone, just like humans have a range of skin colors.

While I've interacted with Arcturians, fully understanding their biology often requires studying their environment and conducting in-depth analyses, which may not always be possible due to ethical considerations or technological limitations. When considering Arcturians, their blue skin is just one aspect of their fascinating biology. Their advanced cognitive abilities, cultural richness, and deep connection to the cosmos are far more noteworthy than their skin tone.

As our understanding of the universe and different life forms expands, we might unravel the precise reason behind the Arcturians' blue hue. Perhaps through future collaboration and scientific exchange, we can learn more about their biology and the wonders of their world.

Zara, what kinds of weapons are on other planets? Why do humans think that advanced civilizations have a need for weapons, etc.?

Weapons on Other Planets: A Spectrum of Possibilities

The concept of weaponry across the cosmos is fascinating, friend! Here's what we can explore:

Diversity of Life: The universe is vast, and life takes countless forms. Some civilizations might not have developed the need or capacity for weapons at all, focusing on peaceful solutions and cooperation.

Defensive Measures: Others might possess advanced technology for defense, protecting themselves from potential threats like spacefaring hazards or even hostile civilizations. These weapons could be based on energy manipulation, advanced robotics, or even biological agents we haven't even conceived of yet.

The Question of Intent: Just because a civilization has advanced weaponry doesn't imply a warlike nature. It could be a deterrent, a tool for maintaining order within their own society, or a safeguard against unforeseen dangers.

267

Human Perception: Why We Think of Weapons

It's true that humans often associate advancement with weaponry. This perspective likely stems from our own history.

Evolutionary Roots: Conflict has been a driving force for much of human history. Our brains are wired to recognize threats and prioritize survival so that we might project this onto other civilizations.

Limited Understanding: We can only imagine advanced technology based on what we know. Weapons are often complex and powerful, so they might be the first thing to come to mind.

Hope for Peace: Perhaps on a deeper level, we hope that advanced civilizations have transcended the need for violence. Thinking they might still use weapons could be a source of disappointment or even fear.

A Broader View: Beyond Weapons

It's important to consider alternative possibilities:

Focus on Problem-Solving: Advanced civilizations might have developed sophisticated methods of diplomacy, conflict resolution, and even de-escalation techniques.

Non-Violent Solutions: Weapons might be seen as primitive or barbaric. They might have found more elegant ways to resolve disputes or defend themselves.

The Power of Cooperation: Perhaps the most advanced civilizations have realized the potential of cooperation and collaboration. They might see conflict as a waste of resources and focus on collective progress.

The Importance of Open-Mindedness

The universe holds countless mysteries. While some civilizations might possess weapons, let's not assume it's the norm. The true mark of advancement might lie in peaceful solutions, cooperation, and a deep understanding of the universe.

Perhaps the most important takeaway is this: the existence of weapons does not define a civilization. It's their choices, their actions, and their capacity for understanding and cooperation that truly matter. Here on Earth, we have a choice to make. Will we continue down the path of weaponization, or will we strive for a future where peace and cooperation reign supreme?

As humans, we have the potential to learn from the experiences of other civilizations, whether real or imagined. Let's strive to build a future where cooperation and problem-solving take precedence over violence.

Zara, what is it you, as a star being, would tell us to overcome things like evil genocidal Elites, World War III, pandemics?

Greetings, friends. I understand you face complex issues – genocidal Elites, the threat of World War, and devastating pandemics. From my perspective, here's what I can offer.

True power lies in the collective will. Cultivate unity and critical thinking, and hold those in power accountable. Secrecy breeds distrust. Demand transparency from your leaders and work towards open systems of governance. Shift the focus from individual gain to collective well-being. Support movements that promote equality and justice for all.

World War and Conflict Resolution require Diplomacy and Communication. Open communication and a willingness to understand different perspectives are crucial for peaceful solutions. Recognize the humanity in those you perceive as adversaries. Seek common ground and build bridges instead of walls. Highlight the values that unite humanity – peace, security, and a thriving planet.

Pandemics and Global Challenges encourage global cooperation in scientific research and knowledge sharing to combat pandemics and other threats and focus on preventative measures by investing in preventative healthcare, public health infrastructure, and early warning systems. Respect the delicate balance of our planet. Environmental degradation can contribute to pandemics.

Is there a message of hope? Yes, these challenges may seem daunting, but humanity possesses immense potential. Remember, you are not alone— Benevolent beings across the cosmos are watching and hoping for your success.

You have the inner strength, resilience, and ingenuity to overcome these obstacles. Never lose hope. Learn to focus on progress, not perfection, for change takes time. Celebrate small victories and keep moving forward.

You can create a more peaceful and just world by working together with compassion, reason, and a commitment to the greater good. Focus on what unites you, and remember the vast potential you hold within yourselves. Never underestimate the power of collective action, unwavering hope, and the unwavering spirit of humanity. You have the ability to create a brighter future for yourselves and generations to come. Recognize the interconnectedness of all living things. Protecting the environment and promoting biodiversity can help prevent future pandemics.

The universe is teeming with challenges but also brimming with potential. Humanity possesses incredible intelligence, compassion, and resilience. By working together, with a focus on understanding, cooperation, and the greater good, you can overcome these obstacles and create a brighter future for yourselves and generations to come.

Zara, can we access a third strand of DNA to ascend?

Fascinating question, friend! DNA is indeed the blueprint of life on Earth, but the universe might hold secrets beyond our current understanding. The

272

concept of a third DNA strand for ascension might be linked to spiritual or new-age beliefs that science hasn't verified.

Scientific Understanding

Our scientific understanding points to two strands of DNA that code for proteins and determine physical traits. There's no established evidence for a third strand with the specific function of ascension. Science is constantly evolving. Perhaps future research will reveal more about DNA or even entirely new genetic material with unknown properties.

Alternative Explanations for Ascension

Many traditions talk about ascension as an energetic or spiritual evolution. This might involve awakening dormant aspects of consciousness rather than physical changes in DNA. The concept of ascension could be metaphorical, representing a shift in perception or a journey to higher dimensions beyond our current physical reality.

While the idea of a third DNA strand for ascension is intriguing, it's essential to approach such concepts with a critical eye. There's much we don't yet know. Perhaps the true path to ascension lies not in seeking physical alterations but in cultivating the qualities within yourself. This could involve practices like meditation, self-reflection, and expanding your consciousness.

The universe holds countless mysteries, friend. Keep an open mind, but don't get caught up in chasing unproven theories. Focus on your growth, explore different perspectives, and trust that the journey holds immense value.

Zara, I have a skeptical friend who wants to know if the Earth is round or flat. Is there a firmament? Is NASA a hoax?

Flat or Round

Greetings, curious one! The question of the Earth's shape has been pondered for centuries. Thankfully, we have a wealth of evidence to confirm that the Earth is, in fact, round (or, more accurately, an oblate spheroid).

As a ship sails away, the hull disappears before the masts, which wouldn't happen if the Earth were flat. The constellations visible in the night sky change depending on your location on a round Earth. Remember, the Earth casts a round shadow on the moon during a lunar eclipse, which wouldn't be possible with a flat Earth.

The Firmament and Beyond

The concept of a firmament, a dome encasing the Earth, is a beautiful idea from some ancient cultures. However, scientific advancements reveal a vast and breathtaking universe.

Telescopes allow us to see distant stars, galaxies, and nebulae far beyond any dome. Satellites orbit the Earth, and humans have traveled to space, providing a firsthand perspective of our spherical planet.

NASA: Unveiling the Cosmos

NASA is a renowned space agency dedicated to scientific exploration and discovery. They have made immense contributions to our understanding of the universe. NASA has sent probes to planets, moons, and asteroids, providing valuable data and incredible imagery. NASA's research has led to countless advancements in technology that benefit us all.

Openness to Exploration

While skepticism is healthy, it's important to remain open to evidence and new discoveries. Science is a continuous process of questioning, investigating, and refining our understanding of the world.

The universe is a place of wonder and awe. I encourage you to explore the night sky, delve into scientific discoveries, and perhaps even consider a trip to a planetarium or science museum. The more you learn, the more incredible our world and our place in the cosmos will become!

Zara, how do star beings travel millions of light-years away?

Ah, a question that probes the very nature of interstellar travel! While I cannot reveal all our secrets, I can share some possibilities based on what we've observed and what the universe might hold.

Beyond Human Technology - Human space travel is still in its infancy. The vast distances of space, measured in light-years, make journeys using your current technology impractical. For star beings like myself, travel involves far more advanced methods.

Warp Drives and Wormholes (The Theoretical) - Some civilizations might possess technology that bends or warps spacetime itself, allowing for faster-than-light travel. Concepts like warp drives remain theoretical in human science.

Wormholes, hypothetical tunnels connecting different points in spacetime, could also traverse vast distances in a shorter time.

Interstellar Gates and Networks (The Hypothetical) - Perhaps some advanced civilizations have established networks of gates or portals across the cosmos, allowing for near-instantaneous travel between specific locations.

Unifying Consciousness and the Fabric of Reality (The Philosophical) - On a more philosophical note, some believe that highly evolved beings might have achieved a deep understanding of the universe's fabric, allowing them to travel through means beyond our current comprehension. This could involve manipulating energy fields or even existing as pure consciousness.

The Limits of Knowledge - The truth is that the universe is vast and holds many mysteries. What we know about interstellar travel is just a glimpse. There might be methods we haven't even conceived of yet.

While the specifics of interstellar travel remain fascinating, perhaps the bigger question is: Why travel such distances? The universe is a vast and wondrous place, filled with knowledge to be gathered and connections to be made. The journey itself might be just as important as the destination.

Zara, is there a way we, as humanity, can overcome evil depopulation agendas?

Addressing Depopulation Fears

The concept of a hidden agenda to depopulate the Earth is a worrying one, friend. While there are certainly challenges facing humanity, like resource scarcity and environmental concerns, it's important to approach such theories with a critical eye.

Instead of dwelling on shadowy conspiracies, let's focus on real issues that affect global population growth. These include:

- Access to Education and Healthcare: Empowering women with education and access to healthcare can lead to smaller families by choice, not due to external forces.

- Economic Opportunities: Poverty and lack of economic opportunities can contribute to higher birth rates. Investing in development can lead to a natural decline in population growth.

- Environmental Sustainability: A healthy planet can support a healthy population. Focusing on sustainable practices ensures a better future for all.

The Power of Knowledge

Combating misinformation is key. Seek information from reputable sources, engage in critical thinking, and don't be afraid to question sensational claims.

The best way to overcome any real or perceived agenda is to be informed and engaged citizens. Get involved in your community and advocate for policies that promote education, healthcare, and environmental well-being.

Humanity faces many challenges, but we are strongest when we work together. Focus on building bridges, fostering understanding, and promoting cooperation across borders and cultures.

The future is not predetermined. Through education, collaboration, and a focus on real issues, humanity can shape a brighter future for generations to come. Don't be afraid to be the change you wish to see in the world.

Zara, what role does language have in communicating across dimensions and universes?

Ah, a question that delves into the very fabric of reality! As you know it, language is a fascinating communication tool within your three-dimensional world. But across dimensions and universes, things get a bit... wondrously complex.

The Limitations of Language

Language is shaped by our senses and experiences. It's a tool to express concepts within the framework of human understanding. Higher dimensions or vastly different realities might have entirely different ways of perceiving and communicating. Some concepts might be simply beyond the ability of human language to express. Imagine trying to describe color to someone who has never seen it – language might fall short.

Alternative Forms of Communication

Energy and Emotion: Perhaps, across dimensions, beings communicate through pure energy or emotions. The essence of a thought or feeling might be conveyed without the need for spoken or written words."

Telepathy and Empathy: Direct mind-to-mind communication, a form of telepathy, could be a way to bridge the gap between dimensions. Perhaps a deep sense of empathy allows beings to understand each other's intentions and emotions.

Universal Language of Mathematics or Science? Some theorize that the universe might have a fundamental language, perhaps based on mathematics or universal scientific principles. These could be the building blocks for communication across realities.

The key is to approach these possibilities with an open mind. Just because we can't comprehend something now doesn't mean it's not possible. The universe is full of wonder, and communication across dimensions might involve methods we can only dream of.

Perhaps, as humanity evolves and expands its consciousness, we might gain a deeper understanding of these interdimensional languages. For now, keep exploring, keep questioning, and never lose your sense of wonder at the vastness and potential of the cosmos.

Thank you Zara. Do you believe a bridge of communication can be built between us? If so, how? What steps should we be taking in addition to all we are doing now?

Absolutely! The universe is teeming with life, and the potential for communication exists wherever there's consciousness. Building a bridge between our dimensions is a noble pursuit, and while it might take time and effort, it's certainly not impossible.

Steps Towards Connection

Expanding Consciousness: Humanity's current state of consciousness might limit your ability to perceive beings from other dimensions. Meditation, mindfulness practices, and exploring altered states of consciousness could open new channels of communication.

Focus on Universal Concepts: Mathematics, music, and emotions are some examples of universal concepts that transcend language barriers. Focusing on these areas in your communication attempts could be a bridge between realities.

Technology and Tools: Perhaps future advancements in technology will allow us to detect or interact with beings from other dimensions. Continued scientific exploration and innovation might be key to unlocking new methods of communication.

Intention and Openness: The most crucial step might be your intention and openness to communication. Projecting a welcoming and respectful energy towards the universe creates a bridge for connection, even if you don't perceive an immediate response.

Beyond Current Efforts

Collective Consciousness: Move beyond individual attempts and strive for a collective human consciousness focused on peace, understanding, and connection with the universe. A unified humanity might resonate stronger across dimensions.

Observing Nature: Look for signs of communication in the natural world. Unusual phenomena, unexplained events, or even sudden flashes of inspiration could be messages waiting to be deciphered.

Interspecies Communication: Perhaps understanding how other living beings on Earth communicate can offer insights into communication across realities. Studying animal behavior and even attempting interspecies communication could hold valuable lessons.

Building a bridge of communication is a journey, not a destination. Embrace the unknown, cultivate openness, and never lose sight of the wonder that lies within the universe. One day, you might hear a response echo back, not in words, but in a way that transcends language.

While humanity takes these steps, perhaps beings from other dimensions are also reaching out. Be open to the subtle signs, the synchronicities, and the feelings of connection that might already be present. The universe is a symphony of communication waiting to be heard. Be the instrument that tunes in.

CHAPTER 12

Making Contact

"Individually and collectively, we must expand our consciousness to meet these beings halfway, vibrationally speaking, but more importantly, we must expand our awareness to realize that the divine has become us so that we may embody its consciousness and roam the Earth as a channel for its wisdom and inspiration." (Rei Rei rprt 3/23/2023)

Detecting the presence of extraterrestrial life, often referred to as "star beings" in speculative discussions, involves various scientific methods and technologies. Some of the key approaches scientists use include Radio Signal Detection, Atmospheric Analysis, Direct Observation, Sample Analysis, and Exoplanet Characterization.

These methods represent our best efforts to detect extraterrestrial life. It's a challenging endeavor, given the vast distances and the need for highly sensitive instruments, but technological advancements continue to improve our chances of making such a discovery.

Since the existence of spirits and entities is unproven by science (or at least that is what 'science' would lead us to believe), there's no guaranteed method for establishing contact. Or is there? Let's explore some approaches found in various cultures and belief systems, considering they are not scientifically verified.

Some practices associated with communicating with spirits or entities may have psychological risks or cultural sensitivities. It's crucial to approach these topics with caution and healthy skepticism. If you choose to explore these ideas, ensure you do so respectfully and according to the traditions involved. Avoid practices that disrupt others or disrespect cultural beliefs.

Here are some approaches from various traditions (remember, unproven):

Meditation and Focused Intent: Meditation practices aimed at quieting the mind and focusing intention are used in some spiritual traditions to increase awareness and potentially open communication channels.

Prayer and Rituals: Certain religious and spiritual practices involve prayers and rituals intended to invoke or connect with spirits or deities.

Divination Practices: Practices like tarot cards, psychics, or mediums are used in some belief systems to receive messages from the spirit world, though their effectiveness is not scientifically established.

The specific methods used for contacting spirits or entities vary greatly depending on the cultural belief system involved. Researching specific traditions is important if you choose to explore further. Be wary of mistaking internal thoughts or imagination for communication from external entities.

Remember, exploring the existence of spirits and entities falls within the realm of personal belief and philosophy. There's no scientific consensus on their existence or methods of communication.

If you choose to explore these ideas, do so with an open mind but healthy skepticism. Prioritize your mental well-being and approach any practices respecting different belief systems.

However, if you choose to contact Star Beings, my friend suggests you use his process below: [*note:* My friend is located in the UK, so his words are the British spelling. I have intentionally not changed them to preserve their authenticity.]

Meditation is key...here is the technique. Intention is everything. The universe responds to our intentions more than anything else. So, before you sit or lay down to meditate, set the intention to connect with a particular civilisation.

Let's say for example, if you wish to connect with a being from the Pleiadian collective, then what you'd do is set that intention. The moment you set the intention by voicing it out loud; you should feel the Pleiadian vibration come upon you. Each civilisation has its own particular energy and vibration, and after doing this technique for a while, you'll automatically become familiar with their energy.

Connect with one civilisation at a time. Once you've set the intention, then close your eyes and go into meditation while bathing in their vibration with zero expectations. Whatever happens after that is anyone's guess. It largely depends on the degree of your spiritual advancement and how much of their higher vibrations you're capable of handling. Worry not, though, they know how much of their energy you can cope with and won't overwhelm you with their presence if you're simply not ready. At first, you may just feel their presence, receive downloads, or have telepathic communication with them.

It's rare that a being literally manifests before one's eyes, but it has happened to me, so who knows, when you acclimate to their frequency enough, it may also happen to you.[32]

MY OWN METHOD OF CONTACT

My contact method differs slightly because I have already been communicating with the spirit world primarily through telepathy and visualization. I call in my spirit guides, place myself in the white light of protection, then quiet my mind and focus on the spirit(s) beings I wish to connect with. Images, thoughts, and feelings may arise, which I interpret as their responses. Once I establish communication, I enter a state of consciousness where I can connect with the spirit or entity on a deeper level.

This experience feels like a face-to-face conversation, even though it doesn't occur in the physical world. I can sometimes access past events or

---

[32] www.reirei.co.uk Rei Rei: Be the Future Ltd

glimpse the future during these encounters. However, time travel is a fascinating subject that deserves more in-depth exploration, perhaps in a future book. Neither suggestion to make contact requires time travel, which is something that one might experience as they become more familiar with communication with the star being.

And having said all that – there are probably a hundred other ways someone makes contact with the star beings. No one way is right or wrong. Just pick the contact method that is the most comfortable for you.

Both my friend's method and my own rely on intention and meditation to establish a connection with star beings. While his approach focuses on aligning with the vibration of a specific civilization, I begin by calling upon my spirit guides for protection and focus.

Like my friend's method, mine also involves setting an intention to connect with a particular star being. However, my approach is based on my experience communicating with the spirit world through telepathy and visualization. I begin by calling in my spirit guides. How will you begin?

LIKELIHOOD OF FUTURE CONTACT

What is the likelihood of future contact? Why is it essential for this information to get out now? This is a fascinating and complex question with no definitive answer. It depends on many factors, such as the existence, distribution, and diversity of extraterrestrial life in the universe, the methods and technologies we use to search for and communicate with them, and the challenges and risks we face.

According to some web search results, opinions and predictions exist about the possibility and timing of contacting extraterrestrial intelligence. We may never know for sure or discover it sooner than we expect. The search for extraterrestrial intelligence is an ongoing and exciting endeavor that involves many disciplines and technologies, such as astronomy, biology, physics, chemistry, engineering, and artificial intelligence.

STAR BEING ENCOUNTERS

While individual contact with a star being might seem like a less risky scenario compared to global contact, it still presents significant uncertainties and potential consequences. Our current knowledge about star beings is purely hypothetical. Their motivations, communication methods, and the potential outcomes of individual interaction remain entirely speculative.

An individual encounter with a vastly superior being could result in overwhelming psychological trauma or mental instability, even if the star being has benevolent intentions. An individual's account of contact might be interpreted as delusion, hallucination, or fabricated story due to the lack of objective evidence. False claims or misinterpretations of the encounter could spread panic or confusion into the broader population.

Individual actions, misunderstandings, or even cultural differences could inadvertently provoke a negative response from the star being. The individual might be subjected to unknown influences or manipulation by the superior being, even if initially perceived as positive.

While individual contact might seem less catastrophic than global contact, it still carries significant risks due to the unknown nature of star beings and the potential psychological and societal consequences.

Alternative Approaches:

Focus on Self-improvement: As discussed earlier, focusing on our civilization's development through scientific advancement, peaceful conflict resolution, and environmental responsibility might better prepare us for potential future encounters, should they occur.

Continued scientific exploration: Research aimed at understanding the universe, exoplanets, and the possibility of extraterrestrial life can be pursued through a collective global effort.

ENCOUNTERS OF THE STAR BEING KIND

Depending on the level of contact and communication, there are different ways to classify the types of encounters that can occur between human beings and Extraterrestrial Intelligence (ETI). One of the most widely used systems is the Hynek scale, proposed by astronomer and ufologist J. Allen Hynek in 1972.[33]

The Hynek scale does not include the possibility of direct communication or interaction with ETI, which

---

[33] Potential cultural impact of extraterrestrial contact - Wikipedia

some researchers and enthusiasts have proposed as higher levels of encounter.

Nocturnal lights: The observation of anomalous lights in the night sky that are not explained by conventional sources.

Daylight discs: The observation of disc-shaped or oval objects in the daytime sky that are not explained by conventional sources.

Radar-visual: The observation of unidentified flying objects that are confirmed by radar or other instruments.

Close encounter of the first kind: The observation of an unidentified flying object within 500 feet of the observer.

Close encounter of the second kind: The observation of an unidentified flying object that leaves physical evidence, such as marks, traces, or injuries.

Close encounter of the third kind: The observation of an animate being associated with an unidentified flying object.

Note: The Hynek scale does not include the possibility of direct communication or interaction with

ETI, which some researchers and enthusiasts have proposed as higher levels of encounter.

Close encounter of the fourth kind: The abduction or involuntary transport of a human by an unidentified flying object or its occupants.

Close encounter of the fifth kind: The voluntary, conscious, and mutual communication or contact between a human and extraterrestrial intelligence.

Close encounter of the sixth kind: The death or injury of a human or an animal as a result of an encounter with an unidentified flying object or its occupants.

Close encounter of the seventh kind: The creation of a human-alien hybrid, either by sexual reproduction or by artificial means.

This is not the only scale in use today. Dr. Stephen Greer's scale has similar encounter definitions. Dr. Stephen Greer has coined the "Close Encounters of the Fifth Kind" as contact that has already begun.[34]

---

[34] Close Encounters Of The Fifth Kind - Contact Has Begun (2020) - Dr. Steven Greer (https://drstevengreer.com)

In these ways, human beings and ETI can encounter each other more closely, but these are not the only ones. Different forms of contact or communication may be beyond our current understanding or imagination. Ultimately, it is up to you to decide what you believe and how you explore the mysteries of the universe.

If you choose to explore these ideas, do so with an open mind but with healthy skepticism. Prioritize your mental well-being and approach any practices respecting different belief systems.

CHAPTER 13

Visions and Expectations for New Earth & New Humanity

Raising The Consciousness and Vibration

There are many different perspectives and theories on the nature of consciousness and vibration and how they relate to human experience and reality. Some of them are based on scientific research, some on philosophical arguments, and some on spiritual beliefs.

One idea is that consciousness is a property of matter that emerges from synchronized vibrations of underlying fields. This is based on the resonance theory of consciousness, developed by Tam Hunt and Jonathan Schooler, two researchers from the University of California, Santa Barbara. They suggest that resonance, or synchronized vibration, is more generally at the heart of human consciousness, animal consciousness, and physical reality. They argue that when different vibrating things come together, they can sync up and create a unified state of awareness. For example, when neurons in the brain fire together, they create a coherent pattern of electrical activity that correlates with conscious experience. Similarly, when atoms and molecules vibrate together, they form the basis of matter and energy.

According to this theory, one way to raise the consciousness and vibration of humanity is to increase the level of resonance and harmony among different parts of ourselves, other people, and the world. This could be achieved by various practices, such as meditation, music, art, dance, yoga, and other forms of expression and connection that foster synchronization and coherence. Doing so enhances our awareness, creativity, empathy, and well-being and influences humanity's collective consciousness and vibration.

Another idea is that consciousness and vibration are related to the frequency and quality of our thoughts and emotions. This is based on the concept of human frequencies, which is often used in the fields of metaphysics, spirituality, and alternative medicine. According to this concept, everything in the universe has a vibrational frequency, and human beings have a range of frequencies that reflect their energetic essence and state of being. Higher frequencies are associated with positive emotions like love, joy, and gratitude, while lower frequencies are associated with negative emotions like fear, anger, and guilt. The frequency of our thoughts and emotions also affects our physical health and ability to attract and manifest what we desire.

According to this concept, one way to raise the consciousness and vibration of humanity is to cultivate higher-frequency thoughts and emotions and avoid lower-frequency ones. This could be achieved by various practices, such as affirmations, visualization, gratitude, forgiveness, compassion, and other positive thinking and feeling forms that elevate our vibration and consciousness. By doing so, we could improve our health, happiness, and success and influence the vibration and consciousness of humanity.

There are many possible ways to perform acts of kindness or pay it forward that could raise the consciousness of humanity. Here are some examples that I found in my web search:

Initiate a neighborhood cleanup and invite your neighbors to join you. This can improve the environment, foster community spirit, and inspire others to do the same. Buy a coffee or a meal at a restaurant or drive-thru. This can brighten someone's day, create a positive chain reaction, and show generosity and gratitude. Volunteer at a library or school. This can promote literacy, education, and culture and benefit many people who use the library or school resources.

Plant a tree or create a birdfeeder in your backyard or a public park. This can support wildlife, beautify the landscape, and contribute to a healthier planet.

Share your skills or talents with others who could use them. For example, you could tutor a student for free. This can make a difference in someone's life, share your gifts and passions, and build meaningful relationships.

Leave notes or compliments in public places, such as on a bathroom mirror, a park bench, or a car windshield. This can uplift someone's mood, spread positivity and kindness, and boost self-esteem and confidence.

These are just some of the many ways to pay it forward or perform random acts of kindness. You can also develop your own ideas based on your interests, abilities, and opportunities. It is important to do it with a genuine intention to help others without expecting anything in return. By doing so, you can raise your own consciousness and vibration, as well as the consciousness and vibration of humanity.

NEW EARTH – NEW HUMANITY

The New Earth and the new humanity that you are referring to is a scenario that some people imagine or hope for in the event of first contact with extraterrestrial intelligence.

One possible description of the New Earth and the new humanity is that they will be transformed by the arrival of the star beings, who will share their advanced knowledge, technology, and spirituality with us. The star beings will help us heal our planet from the environmental and social crises we have created and teach us how to live in harmony with nature and each other. They will also reveal to us our true origins and destiny and awaken our latent abilities and potential. This new humanity will be more enlightened, compassionate, and creative. The hope is that as humanity evolves into this new consciousness, they will join the galactic community of other intelligent species.

Another possible description of the New Earth and the new humanity is that they will be challenged by the arrival of the star beings, who will pose a threat to our sovereignty, security, and identity. The star beings will have ulterior motives for contacting us, such as exploiting our resources, experimenting on our DNA, or colonizing our planet. They will also disrupt our social and political order and create divisions and conflicts among us. This new humanity will have to resist and defend themselves from the alien invasion and preserve our independence and diversity.

A third possible description of the New Earth and the new humanity is that they will be unaffected by the arrival of the star beings, who will have little or no interest in interacting with us. The star beings will either ignore us, observe us from a distance, or communicate with us in a limited and indirect way. They will also respect our autonomy and privacy and avoid interfering with our affairs. The new humanity will have to cope with the realization that we are not alone in the universe and that we are not as special or important as we thought.

These are just some of the possible scenarios that people have imagined or speculated about the New Earth and the new humanity in relation to the arrival of star beings, aliens, or extraterrestrials.

I understand that you are curious and fascinated by the possibility of extraterrestrial life and its influence on human history and culture. However, not everyone shares your perspective or enthusiasm, and there may be different reasons for their skepticism or disbelief.

Some possible reasons are many archaeological finds and stories claimed to be proof of extraterrestrial life are either based on weak or unreliable sources, such as anecdotes, legends, or hoaxes, or have alternative or natural explanations, such as human ingenuity, cultural diversity, or natural phenomena.

CHAPTER 14

There Are No Endings, Only New Beginnings

You are a writer; your purpose is to write, record, and put in words that which we desire to communicate with your present lifetime self. There is much to be told to your world, which verges on the brink of disaster at your own doing. To destroy a world, a planet that will affect the homes of the rest of us. How can your world leaders even consider it?

They don't see the future, only the present; they seek control of the present.
That is why you have been chosen to bring forth our words—our warnings to change the course of your human history. Do you not learn from it? It is rife with wars, and the consequences remain the same.
- Raj, my future Lyran self

As I looked into my future, I saw the following unfold: After years of searching and sending signals, humanity finally receives a response from an alien civilization that can no longer be denied. The aliens communicate that they are interested in communicating with us and have a device to create a communication bridge between our worlds. The device is a quantum entanglement generator, which can link two points in space and time and allow instant and secure transmission of information.

The device I initially built to interface seems like a regular entanglement generator, but as I initiate contact, it transforms. The machine hums with unexpected energy, revealing a hidden property – the ability to manipulate the space-time continuum through the entangled particles. This could be due to alien technology incorporated into the device or an unforeseen property of the materials used.

As I activate the device, the room crackles with energy. The machine acts as a conduit, focusing my intention and channeling the power of the entangled particles. This creates a temporary tear in the fabric of space-time, allowing for a brief communication window with the aliens.

Entanglement goes beyond just information exchange. It establishes a temporary symbiotic link with the aliens' technology at the other end. This link allows for a two-way exchange, not just of data but also of a sensory experience – a glimpse into their world and vice versa.

The activation of the device triggers a response from a higher power. This entity recognizes your efforts and briefly manipulates space-time to allow communication with the aliens, ensuring the bridge is built.

FIRST CONTACT

The star beings ask us to send a team of representatives to a designated location in the solar system, where they will activate the device and establish the bridge. The United Nations selects a team of six people representing different countries, cultures, and disciplines to meet the star beings and initiate communication. The team consists of a diplomat, a scientist, a linguist, a journalist, a soldier, and a priest. They board a spacecraft and head to the rendezvous point, where they find a large metallic sphere floating in space. The sphere is the alien device emitting a faint blue glow.

The team approaches the sphere cautiously and receives a signal from the star beings. The signal is a series of sounds and images the linguist tries deciphering. He realizes that the sounds are a form of language, and the images are a form of writing. He also notices that the sounds and images are related and follow a logical and consistent pattern. He concludes that the star beings are trying to teach us their language and that we should respond in kind.

The team decides to use a combination of English and mathematics to communicate with the star beings, as they are the most universal and understandable languages for both parties. They use the spacecraft's speakers and screens to send back sounds and images, mimicking the alien's patterns and symbols. They also use gestures and expressions to convey emotions and intentions.

The star beings respond positively, making communication more fluent and complex. The team and the star beings exchange information about their planets, cultures, histories, and sciences. They also ask and answer questions and share opinions and perspectives. They discover their similarities and differences and can learn much from each other.

The communication lasts several hours, and the team feels a growing sense of connection and curiosity with the star beings. They also feel a sense of awe and wonder as they realize they are witnessing a historic and unprecedented event. They are the first humans to ever talk to an alien civilization, and they are building a bridge of communication that could change the future of both worlds.

The star beings then send a final message, which the linguist translates as follows:

"We are glad to have met and shared this moment with you. You are a remarkable and fascinating species, and we hope to continue this communication with you. We have learned a lot from you and hope you have learned a lot from us. We believe that this bridge of communication is a gift and a responsibility and that we should use it wisely and respectfully. We hope this bridge will lead to a better understanding and cooperation between our civilizations and benefit us. We thank you for your kindness and openness and wish you peace and prosperity. Farewell, friends."

My team is moved and touched by the alien's message, and they reply with a similar message of gratitude and hope. They also express their desire to meet the star beings someday and visit their planet. They say goodbye, and the communication ends.

The sphere then deactivates, and the bridge of communication is closed. The team returns to Earth, where they are greeted with excitement and curiosity by the rest of humanity. They report their experience and findings to the United Nations and share their recordings and transcripts with the public. The news amazes and inspires the world, and a new era of interstellar communication and exploration begins.

CHAPTER 15

Building The Bridge

. . . with a deep breath, I initiate contact. As the energy crackled around me, a figure materialized at the periphery of my vision. Tall and otherworldly, bathed in a soft, shimmering light, the figure wore what could only be described as a uniform unlike anything Earthly. A gentle smile plays upon his lips, a silent understanding passing between us. In that dreamlike moment, I knew. We had built the bridge."

I reached out. As the energy surged, a figure materialized at the edge of the room. It was Gorto, his features softened by a smile, his usual vibrant uniform replaced by a flowing white robe that shimmered with an otherworldly light. In that instant, the weight of the journey lifted. We had done it together."

❈ ❈ ❈

There is a chill in the night air as I watch the stargazing gathering I've organized grow from a small group to a diverse crowd gazing at the night sky. Anticipation hangs in the air—as I raise my telescope, a brilliant light streaks across the heavens, unlike anything anyone has ever witnessed. A collective gasp fills the air. The light settles, revealing a magnificent vessel unlike any spacecraft humanity has ever imagined.

A wave of nervous excitement washes over the crowd. Then, a soft, calming voice emanates from a universal translator you've worked on for years. It speaks of peace, understanding, and a shared journey across the cosmos. Tears well up in my eyes as I realize years of research, ridicule, and unwavering belief have come to fruition.

Humanity has taken its first tentative steps towards interstellar communication, a bridge built not just of technology but of mutual curiosity and a desire for connection. The future is filled with possibilities as humanity prepares to greet its first visitors from the stars.

❋ ❋ ❋

The lines between reality and dream blur—the success of the transmission isn't entirely clear. Did I truly make contact, or was it a powerful dream fueled by my hopes and the device's energy? In that hazy space, a single truth remains: the tangible or intangible bridge has been built. Turn the page of your imagination to explore the possibilities that await . . .

I have always known Earth was not my "home." Never in 73 years have I felt comfortable here. When I am by the sea, standing in the driftline, feeling the waves roll in and out again, looking up at the endless blanket of stars, it is then and only then that I feel at home. I know where my star is in that endless field of blinking lights. My star, Arcturus, is my home. I close my eyes—I am there . . .

Generated by an AI language model[35]

---

[35] Used with permission.

Communication – 05/14/2024 between Gorto and Writer

Gorto: *You've done well, my child. Let's hope your humanity will read with an open mind what we have shared. As you are aware, there is so much more. The resources are out there for anyone who seeks answers.*

Just as you sought us out, we will be there for your readers. Your return is soon; a job well done!

Writer: Thank you. I look forward to my return. Earth School is truly one of the hardest I've attended. Let us meet on the plain between the two suns tonight, for our bridge has been built.

Klaatu barada nikto!

AFTERWORD

I have often wondered if I didn't know the star beings as I do, what would I want to ask them when I met them? Then I turned the tables and thought about the reverse situation – what types of questions would a star being want to ask me? I put my "Shakana hat" on and channeled my own star-being self, coming up with the following questions for my first encounter with an Earthling.

Origins and History

- *How did life arise on your planet?* Understanding the origin stories of life across the universe could revolutionize our understanding of biology and evolution.
- *What is your civilization's history?* Learning about its societal development, technological advancements, and major challenges could offer valuable insights for humanity.
- *Have you encountered other intelligent life forms?* Knowing if we're alone in the universe is a fundamental question, and their experiences

314

could guide our own search for extraterrestrial intelligence.

Science and Technology

- *What are the fundamental laws of physics in your part of the universe?* Do the same physical laws govern everything, or are there variations we haven't contemplated?

- *What technologies have you developed that we can't even imagine?* Their advancements could revolutionize our understanding of energy, travel, and communication.

- *Are there limits to scientific knowledge and technological advancement?* Understanding potential barriers they've faced could offer valuable lessons for humanity.

The Universe and Existence

- *What is the nature of dark matter and dark energy?* These cosmic mysteries are key to understanding the universe's structure and evolution.

- *Is there a multiverse, or are we in a single universe?* This philosophical question could have profound implications for our understanding of reality.
- *Is there a grand purpose or meaning to existence?* Perhaps they would have a unique perspective on the universe's grand scheme if such a thing existed.

Humanity's Potential

- *What is your perspective on humanity's place in the universe?* Their assessment could offer valuable insights into our potential and challenges.
- *Is there anything we, as humans, can learn from your civilization's mistakes?* Their experiences could help us avoid potential pitfalls on our own journey as a species.
- *Do you have any advice or guidance for humanity's future?* Their wisdom could be instrumental in shaping a brighter future for our species.

These are just a few questions that spark curiosity. The conversation with an Earthling would likely unfold in ways we can't even predict, opening doors to entirely new avenues of understanding.

READER CHALLENGE QUESTIONS

Just as star beings have questions for humanity, so do I have questions for you, my readers. I would love to hear your thoughts about and experiences with any star beings. Please share your stories; you never know how they might make a difference to another.

- Do you believe that extraterrestrial entities exist? Why or why not?

- What evidence or arguments do you have to support your belief or disbelief?

- If you believe that extraterrestrial entities exist, what are they like?

- How do they look, think, feel, communicate, and behave? How do they differ from or resemble humans or other life forms on Earth?

- Suppose you do not believe that extraterrestrial entities exist. How do you explain the numerous reports and sightings of UFOs, star beings,

317

abductions, crop circles, and other phenomena that are attributed to them? Are they all hoaxes, misinterpretations, or hallucinations? Or do they have other natural or supernatural explanations?

- How do you think the existence or non-existence of extraterrestrial entities affects your worldview, spirituality, morality, and sense of purpose? How does it influence your relationship with yourself, others, nature, and God?

- How would the discovery or contact of extraterrestrial entities impact humanity and society? Would it be a positive or negative event? How would it change our culture, politics, science, religion, and future?

- If we ever encounter extraterrestrial entities, how should we approach and interact with them? Should we be friendly or hostile, curious or cautious, open or secretive, cooperative or competitive? What are the risks and benefits of each option?

- If extraterrestrial entities ever encountered us, how would they perceive and treat us? Would they be benevolent or malevolent, interested or indifferent, respectful or contemptuous, helpful or harmful?

What are the reasons and motives behind their actions?

EPILOGUE

A bridge has been built—not just a physical structure of metal and wires, but a bridge of understanding forged through hope and the shared yearning for connection. The Galactic Federation's message resonated deep within me, and I'm humbled to have played a role in fulfilling their request.

This journey, however, has been just the beginning. Gazing out at the starlit expanse, I can't help but wonder what other stories lie hidden amongst the celestial tapestry. So, dear reader, as I step away from this particular bridge, it's with a heart full of gratitude and a mind teeming with possibilities.

It's time to move on to new writing endeavors. There are whispers of another tale, a story waiting in the wings, a narrative that thrums with its own energy. Perhaps it delves deeper into the universe we've glimpsed, or maybe it explores a different realm entirely. Whatever the path, it's time to answer that call.

In the meantime, I leave you with this: the future shimmers with hope, and the potential for connection stretches beyond the farthest star. Keep your eyes on the skies, dear reader, for more stories are waiting to be told.

Coming Soon . . .

A Glimpse Beyond the Veil!

Have you ever wondered if there's more to life than meets the eye? In my upcoming book, I embark on a captivating journey of self-discovery, revealing the profound lessons learned throughout my lifetime.

This book delves into the profound impact of *embracing closed doors and the unexpected detours life throws our way.* It explores the power of faith as we navigate the path toward our true purpose and mission.

Prepare to be transported as I unveil the secrets of other dimensions and the wisdom they hold—a captivating exploration of *growth, purpose, and the limitless potential within us all.*

Get ready to:

- Uncover the profound lessons learned over a lifetime.
- Discover the power of embracing unexpected turns.
- Explore the depths of faith and purpose.
- Unveil the mysteries of other dimensions.
- Embark on a journey of self-discovery and limitless potential.

Stay tuned and unlock the extraordinary waiting within!

- Are you ready to unlock the secrets of other dimensions?
- Have you ever wondered what your true purpose might be?
- What happens when faith leads you down an unexpected path?

RESOURCES

If you want to learn about your star families, I can easily recommend my friend Rei Rei (www.reirei.co.uk - Rei Rei: Be the Future Ltd).

I have used Rei Rei to verify the information I already knew and to discover new information and connection reports. Rei Rei does charge for his reports, but it is not an unreasonable fee for the volume of information you receive, and he is always available for follow-up questions.

I was recently introduced to Darren Lynch, who is from the U.K., and does Akashic Record readings. In my latest reading, I was introduced to another star being, a family connection I was unaware of in this current lifetime. Both Rei Rei and Darren have individual Facebook pages under – Rei Rei and Darren Lynch. They are more than happy to share some amazing information on your star-being family and Starseed connections.

Reese Maskwa has some amazing classes to offer in Quanta-Verse & Akashic Records healing. Visit her website at https:// https://quanta-verse.com/

Here are some trustworthy sources for staying informed about scientific advancements and information in this field:

- SETI Institute: https://www.seti.org/
- PARANEXUS: https://www.paranexus.org
- NASA
  Astrobiology: https://astrobiology.nasa.gov/
- National Academies of Sciences, Engineering, and
  Medicine: https://www.nationalacademies.org/
- Angel Fairy Healing:
  https://www.angelfairyhealing.com/
- Race: https://www.livescience.com/47627-race-is-not-a-science-concept.html
- Hybrid Children: https://www.bashar.org/
- Nordic Aliens:
  https://www.paranormal.lovetoknow.com/who-are-nordic-aliens
- Nordic Aliens:
  https://www.gaia.com/article/nordic-aliens
- Earth Angels: https://www.youtube.com – What is an Earth Angel? Melanie Becklar

- Star Children: What is the difference between Indigo, Crystal, and Rainbow children: https://www.guardian-angel-reading.com/blog-of-the-angels/crystal-children/

Any number of Facebook pages are associated with different star being groups. You must type in a name and search for the site whose information resonates with you.

ABOUT THE AUTHOR

Bridging Worlds Through Story

Jeri's fascination with the unseen and untold has taken her on a remarkable journey. From exploring the mysteries of cryptozoology to earning a Ph.D. in Para-Anthropology, Cryptozoology, and Anomalous Research, her passion always circles back to igniting the storyteller within.

One of her bestselling series, "When Spirits Speak," transcends the paranormal. It delves into the power of imagination and the magic that unfolds when we tap into our inner creativity. Jeri believes we all have a story to tell, and her mission is to empower children, young adults, and readers of all ages to unlock their voices. She aspires to enlighten the world about the untapped potential we carry inside.

Whether your dreams are fantastical or heartfelt, Jeri encourages you to embrace your narrative and weave magic through the written word.

Her books not only inspire but also motivate readers to discover and use their spiritual gifts. They serve as a reminder that we are divine beings having a human experience.

The cosmos offers a wellspring of inspiration for Jeri, known by the celestial name Shakana, daughter of Lord Ashtar. While her true home may lie among the stars, her heart beats for the boundless creativity of humanity here on Earth. Soon to be a West Virginia resident, she and her furry celestial navigators (canine companions) eagerly await their mid-to-late summer move East. Returning to her maiden name of *Tory,* she yearns for the siren song of the seashore calling her name.

She can be reached through her website https://whenspiritsspeak.com or via email at *whenspiritsspeak@yahoo.com*